Corporate Wives—
CORPORATE
CASUALTIES ?

Also by ROBERT SEIDENBERG

Mind and Destiny   1964
(with Hortence S. Cochrane)

Marriage in Life and Literature 1970
(reprinted in paperback under the
title *Marriage Between Equals*)

Corporate Wives—
CORPORATE
CASUALTIES?

ROBERT SEIDENBERG, M.D.

amacom

A Division of American Management Associations

© 1973 AMACOM

A division of American Management Associations, New York.
All rights reserved. Printed in the United States of America.

International standard book number: 0-8144-5331-7
Library of Congress catalog card number: 73-77954

First printing

To

ROSE and JOSEPH SEIDENBERG

by a grateful son

PREFACE

CONTRARY TO WHAT some might anticipate, this is a book without villains. In a period when it is both fashionable and profitable to attack our corporate Goliaths, I cannot in good conscience follow in that vein. Similarly I hold no devil theory about my fellow husbands. Instead I direct my animus against the existential traps into which so many of us unwittingly and helplessly fall. What I say is that we can all do better if freed from the incapacitating baggage of outmoded compulsions.

Corporations have been less than kind to women. Their cruelty has been as much out of *machismo* as malice. The question they ask first is, How can the wife be of help to the company? Minimally, the just question should be: Ask not what a wife can do for the corporation but what she can do for herself.

Until recently we have accepted facile explanations and rationalizations of disintegrative behavior of spouses and children on the basis of inherent weakness or inferiority. Psychology most conveniently supplied the rhetoric—words like neurosis or psychosis—to hide inordinate stresses and injustices as a result of repeated uprooting in the name of progress and opportunity.

Children, helpless to communicate their feelings and frustrations, were looked upon as behavior problems, prone to delinquency and drugs. Only the end results were perceived but none of the oppressions visited upon them by a life of nomadism imposed by otherwise well-intentioned corporations and fathers.

But now we have begun to shift our focus and to see the true nature of some of the problems of the corporate wife. Wives suffer because their identities and sense of self-worth are shattered by continual moves. Unlike their husbands, for them there is neither opportunity nor energy to reestablish their importance and authority in new communities. Arduously built credentials cannot be readily transferred again and again; after a while, one doesn't even bother. It is then that many begin to feel less than human and become ripe for tripping, tippling, and tranquilization.

The stated complaint is invariably loneliness. This is the word to cover myriad unexpressed and unexpressible feelings of frustration, disappointment, and disillusionment. It really means not only being *left alone* by husbands and fathers but *left behind,* excluded from those interests and challenges needed by all beings of intelligence. It means being torn from friends, confidantes, and constituents. To be separated from people and activities that make one feel worthy makes one feel both lonely and empty. There is nothing pathological or clinical about this—every poet, or other sensitive person, knows all about the feeling.

Corporate America must vigorously enlist the talents of women as competent human beings rather than as playthings and servants. The lily-white male corporate image should be a shameful sight to those dedicated to both fair play and democracy. The social audit, which David Rockefeller suggests, is long overdue. Would it really diminish a truly secure corporation (or man) to be directed by a competent woman? The times are ripe for women "at the top"; sexism today has no rationale or logic to it.

For the corporate executive, being liberated from the yoke of *machismo* may pay not only the dividend of improved interpersonal relations, but the bonus of added years to his own life—for the result may well be softer arteries rather than the feared softheadedness.

To Stephen MacDonald of *The Wall Street Journal* should go the credit for putting this project into motion by seeing the value and pertinence of my essay that he published as "Dear Mr. Success: Consider Your Wife." But it was Thomas Gannon of the American Management Associations who provided the convincing arguments that this thesis was of sufficient importance and interest to warrant a book. To him and his associates, therefore, must go the credit for its creation and production.

It is impossible to thank adequately the scores of people, men and women, with whom I have corresponded on this issue. For reasons of privacy many of them must remain anonymous. In every chapter the reader will see the invaluable contribution they have made. Similarly I am indebted to the executive officers of our leading corporations for freely and graciously providing information about their personnel practices and procedures.

After the data were gathered, Karen DeCrow, graduate of the Syracuse College of Law and a leading feminist of our day, gave tremendous aid both in editing the manuscript and in providing up-to-date knowledge on the status and thrust of the women's movement. To Marion Cole what can I say for devoted typing and stenography as she did for *Mind and Destiny* and *Marriage in Life and Literature* in the past decade?

I express my deep gratitude to editors Natalie Meadow and Sally Gran who put it all together. I have become writer enough to recognize what a blessing editors' contributions can be.

Robert Seidenberg, M.D.

CONTENTS

PROLOGUE

Dear Mr. Success:

CONSIDER YOUR WIFE

The impetus for this book came from an essay of mine called "Dear Mr. Success: Consider Your Wife," which appeared in The Wall Street Journal *of February 7, 1972. On reading it many felt that the subject merited further study and exposition. That piece is reproduced here.*

THERE IS MUCH to be said for being on the move—it prevents stagnation, promotes adventure, and offers prospects for new opportunities. For many political, religious, and economic refugees, it has meant a new life. For the male in corporate America, it has most often meant challenge and advancement. The man who will not move becomes the deadwood of the company, no longer worthy of serious consideration for top executive positions.

In the moves for enhancement, wives and children usually assent dutifully. Yet such changes of community can have deleterious effects on "helpmates"—the wives who come along for the benefit of their husbands and their families. The hardship for the woman (besides the physical tasks of the move, generally left to the weaker sex) is found in losses that accrue to her in particular, losses not only of friends or neighbors with whom she has grown comfortable but also of status that has come from accomplishment in the community where she resides— the name that she has made for herself in the social and societal sphere if not in a professional role.

In contrast to her husband, whose credentials are easily transferable, her identity as a person, apart from being a wife or a mother, is rarely transferable. In a new community she finds that she must create one all over again. It is starting from the bottom once more for most mobile wives—for some again and again. Often they become defeated people, casualties of "success." They are seen clinically during their third and fourth decades of life chronically depressed, lacking in hope or desire, frequently addicted to alcohol, tranquilizers, and barbiturates.

The following case history shows the effects of this existential problem involving a married couple who did "all the right things"—that is, they followed the American dream of success and achievement, as well as conforming with the gender-role-playing expectations of man and woman.

A 38-year-old woman came for therapy following what was apparently a suicide attempt with an overdose of barbiturates and alcohol. She had remnants of former attractiveness but was now quite plump and puffy. In high school she had been chosen queen of the State Fair and was very popular. She was an only child, and her middle-class parents gave her "everything"; yet she remained gracious and temperate and was never thought of as spoiled. After high school she matriculated at a school of nursing, where again dates were plentiful and she excelled in her work.

She met and subsequently fell in love with a young law student, quite handsome, with a promising future. There were no religious or ethnic disparities; both sets of parents looked on approvingly. They were married while he was attending law school and she was completing her nursing training. Finishing her education first, she was able to obtain immediate work at the university hospital, where again she was both accepted and praised. She was there for two years. When her husband completed law school, they moved to another city, where he was appointed a junior partner in a prominent and prestigious law firm.

She on the other hand was pregnant, much to the satisfaction of the entire family. Thereafter she was to attend to her new family. As a specialist in an emerging field in great demand, her husband made meteoric progress in the new city. His prestige, social status, and income were quite exceptional for a young man. She was contented at home; in a short time there were two children.

When she openly wondered about the possibility of keeping her hand in nursing, her husband as well as her parents indicated that there was really no need for it: it might be an embarrassment to the husband. After all, the wife of a successful man shouldn't be handling bedpans. She offered no resistance—there was too much going for them.

She made friends easily and ascended the social ladder independently of her husband's status. She became president of the garden club, was the star of local dramatic productions, became a leader in the Junior League. They complemented each other in success—the couple everyone envied. And a romantic spirit persisted. Yes, there were rounds of country club dances and parties, wild and otherwise, with ubiquitous drinking, but intemperance was at the time a problem more for him than for her. She was known not only as the wife of a successful young man but as a person in her own right.

It was in this setting and circumstance that he was sought out as a full partner in a metropolitan law firm. The offer held forth not only a large income but also unique political opportunities. He was elated.

The good news, however, was met for the first time in their marriage by a sense of doubt on her part. He overcame this with reassurances of how great it would be for everyone. She was unconvinced but was hardly in a position to undo such an advantage. Her parents persuaded her that she should not obstruct her husband. He was disappointed in her slight resistance, interpreting it as a breach of loyalty—something new in their relationship.

The move was made, a new home purchased, children were placed in the right schools, proper country club and church joined. However, while he continued climbing she seemed to have lost her former zest. She tried to make the social contacts expected of her, but she was now new—low person on the totem pole. The social climate was kindest to old, established families; women were alumnae of exclusive Eastern schools. Although she was accepted into the membership of various organizations, it was quite apparent to her that unlike his, her credentials were specious, that she would be tolerated but would receive none of the adulation that she had known.

She became increasingly withdrawn. Her children were now grown and away at school and seemed to do very well without her. Predictably as she withdrew she used alcohol and barbiturates increasingly, which in turn made social and service organizations more difficult to attend. She became determined to return to nursing despite the feelings of her husband. But then the problem of licensing in a different state arose. Refresher courses became a requirement, but her drinking made this impossible.

When she appeared for therapy, she had been drinking for three years. Cajoling, threats, and abusiveness by her husband had had no salutary effect. She had been sent out of town for three months for residential therapy. Her husband preferred that she be treated out of the city "to try to keep the whole thing as hidden as possible." She was referred to me from the hospital. The husband, however, had grave reservations about having his family affairs known to any psychiatrist locally. "Allowing" her to come to me for help was a concession on his part that he made with great misgivings.

What came out in treatment? A docile, timid, fear- and guilt-ridden person presented herself, for she had "let everyone down." She had been

3

a disappointment to her parents and a burden to her husband. Everyone makes moves; why couldn't she? Wasn't she weak and ungrateful? All the women she knew would give anything to have such a loving and successful husband. Her parents in their less generous moments called her selfish and spoiled; when they felt charitable they called her mentally ill.

As therapy continued it became increasingly apparent that this woman had had excessive demands placed on her more-than-adequate resources. She was indeed responding to the impossible task of rebuilding an identity for the second or third time. She had simply run out of gas. No one around her either understood or could perceive the social and psychological burden imposed on her.

Consequently she now had little personal identity. All the parties that she had given, all the successful affairs that she had arranged were in no one's memory. These were all things that people had to experience and could not be told about. The "credit" was now lost.

The irony of the situation was compounded by the fact that not husband, parents, nor friends would concede that she even suffered a loss by the move, which made her feel that she was all the more unreasonable. A timid person, she had never known the tactics of rebellion or social action. Her role was one of submission and obeisance, of which alcoholism, drug taking, and suicide are conventional derivatives.

Since therapy was not producing the results that he was hoping for, the husband forbade her to come any more. On her own she sought help from a social agency and joined Alcoholics Anonymous. Two years after the termination of therapy with me, she called. She volunteered the information that she was doing fairly well, attributing gains through her work with AA—real anonymity. And she was living apart from her husband. There is no indication that she has been active in the community other than in Alcoholics *Anonymous*.

Nothing quite fails like success. It is likely that this woman would not have suffered culture shock if she had not attained heightened status before the move. The world seems plagued today with the curse of rising expectations—we never like to be, or take, less than before. Yesterday's victories do not console but only whet the appetite. And there is Camus's warning: every achievement is an enslavement.

It is also fair to reflect that in such an instance the demands of conventional marriage, with its automatic definition of roles, might become a most burdensome cross to bear, especially since all the rules of law and society favor the male partner when a divergent interest between husband and wife arises. The husband in the situation just described cannot be reproached since he was acting within the legal and societal rights of his role: precedent dictates that the wife follow the husband in his need for achievement.

There may, however, be a moral responsibility toward a "loved" one. The writer Anaïs Nin observes: "The essential difficulty I see in relationships around me is that the women, the wives, are willing and ready to help their husbands to fulfill their desires, their objectives, their development or careers. But in few of the husbands do I see the same helpfulness. There is a fear that the development of woman will make her less of a wife, a mate, that they might lose her."[1]

Clearly the patient played by the rules since she did accede to his wishes and made the move that was unfavorable for her, or so she thought. In game-theory concepts her disaffection then represented a sabotage of the arrangement. By dutifully following her husband, she saved herself from the legal and psychological penalties of desertion, but by becoming dysfunctional and obstructive to his new position, she registered her protest in the strongest way open to her. She achieved the effect of at one and the same time following and flouting the rules that had become unacceptable to her in a new decade of her life.

If one must discover the tragic flaw in this patient, she must be faulted for leaving her profession in the beginning, thus depriving herself of the residual power for changes that had to be made later. She was entirely too docile and submissive here, sadly responding of course to the normal upbringing of every girl of her class by placing love of husband before any personal ambitions and strivings.

And yet, in all fairness to her, can she be faulted for doing the right things? Instead perhaps we in the helping professions might profitably reexamine the process of daughter rearing and at the same time suggest remedies for societal inequities that create such existential dilemmas.

Must a woman continue to depend on her husband's good nature and charity in such matters, or cannot better rules be devised to allow for a confrontation on terms of equality? It is indeed ironic that the *home*maker should, under the law as well as ironclad custom, have no right of *domicile*.

The human spirit is apparently such that it does not take easily to diminution or anonymity once it has known better things. Even safety and security do not suffice where matters of personal worthiness and identity are the issues. Charles Reich reflects on what is perhaps the inordinate importance placed on credentials in our society: "In a world where men are recognized only by their credentials, to lose credentials is to cease being a human being."[2]

Agreeing with this statement in general, some, however, would substitute the word "persons" for "men."

PART I

The Trauma of Transfers

DO CORPORATE WIVES HAVE SOULS?

> *When one is uprooted, transplanted, there is a temporary withering.*
>
> ANAIS NIN

FOR THE PAST 20 YEARS, I have written essays on psychological and sociological subjects that have appeared in national scientific and lay periodicals. Never before has a response been so extensive and enthusiastic as to the one on uprooting, "Dear Mr. Success: Consider Your Wife," which appeared in *The Wall Street Journal* and is reproduced in the Prologue of this book.

The essay apparently hit a chord with women and men all over the country who have been suffering silently and privately. In trying to understand the dilemma they are in, they have been blaming themselves and burying the pain and anxiety of purported personal inadequacy as well as they can, using crutches of alcohol, tranquilizers, and other palliatives. They have invariably felt that they should be able to take all the moves and displacements with equanimity, not realizing that there are indeed human limitations beyond which people sink into despair and even illness. The essay indicated that this is indeed both a common problem and a human one. And although there can be great pride in dealing with and overcoming hardships, endurance is not endless; a toll is eventually exacted.

Evidence is mounting to substantiate the observation that moving in America has a deleterious effect, particularly on women. Drs. Myrna M. Weissman and Eugene S. Paykel of the Yale University School of Medicine studied a group of depressed women in New Haven, Connecticut, and found that although women themselves did not relate their depressive symptoms to recent moves, this temporal relationship was quite significant. These investigators suggest that the complaints of financial problems, increased loneliness, heightened marital friction, difficulties

9

with children, career frustrations, and identity confusion were by-products of "faulty adaptation to the stresses and changes created by moving."[1] The authors speculate that these women did not associate their symptoms with moving because it is such an accepted part of American life that they internalized their stresses and blamed themselves. Weissman and Paykel are convinced that the stressful effects of American geographic mobility have been underestimated, that moving often places inordinate demands on the individual to adapt and raises continued challenges to identity. They conclude that although many people move each year with no problems or only transient ones, a substantial number do experience incapacitating suffering.

There are many scholarly treatises and general writings on the problems of uprooting. The historian Oscar Handlin has told us about the vicissitudes of the waves of immigrants who came to America to start new lives. John Steinbeck's *The Grapes of Wrath* deals with the westward migration of poor white Americans during the years of the Great Depression. Anna Freud, in England, has described the plight and psychology of displaced children during World War II. More recently Robert Coles has written poignantly about a largely unseen segment of uprooted children of migrant black farm workers in America. And although not primarily concerned with social issues, psychoanalytic literature has always concerned itself with the consequences of separation and object loss.

There is, however, surprisingly little in the literature that treats geographic moves and changes that nonwretched people make or are forced to make and that prove to be detrimental or even catastrophic. The subject of this chapter is the wife who must follow her upward-reaching husband, an act by ordinary standards not generally considered to be particularly traumatic. And the thesis of this book is that when husband and wife adhere to their traditional roles, the conventional expectations arising from these roles demand exorbitant renunciations from the women. These excessive renunciations—not personal immaturities or childhood problems—are enough to account for the grave consequences that accrue.

This is not to discount or denigrate the importance of personal history and background for any complete evaluation of a person. A company physician tending an executive's wife may be quite correct in diagnosing her depression as a change-of-life symptom due to hormonal imbalance rather than seeing her as a social casualty of corporate America. The crucial point is that in the inevitable moves of successful businessmen, while the male's identity is usually enhanced, the female's is shredded because of the vast inequity between the one and the other in ability to transfer credentials.

The tradition of the wife's automatically moving with her husband (and his tribe) is exemplified in Biblical Ruth's pledge to her new mother-in-law: "Whither thou goest, so goeth I." The law of our times expects the wife to follow her husband according to his desires and needs. He clearly has the "choice of domicile," meaning that if the wife does not follow, she can no longer claim support from him; it is assumed that she has deserted him and/or the family. This "desertion" also has ramifications in her civil rights. For instance she cannot exercise her right to vote or run for office in any area other than where her husband has established domicile. This is indeed a unique interpretation of the term *desertion,* which in the popular sense connotes some kind of running away or abandonment; for a woman, living by different and inferior rules, "deserts" if she remains. The parallel that comes to mind is a soldier who may be thought of as deserting if he is ordered to the front but stays behind in the staging area.

In some states there are a few protective provisions for a wife. For example she may not be forced to move if the husband changes to a job where his income is decreased; even so, if he can show that he is bettering himself, the wife must accompany him. As to a husband's moving because of a wife's job, the law says nothing, this apparently being a situation either unheard of or beneath judicial consideration.

That all is not well with those who play conventional roles was reported by Lois Wyse, who found dissatisfaction among the wives of successful executives. These women did not aspire to careers of their own. The pertinent finding was that "Unhappiness increased as a husband's recognition in business increased."[2] The plight of the corporate wife is described by Charles Reich as follows: "Wives of middle-class professional men occupy a particularly questionable position; well educated and highly intelligent, they are forced into a position in which they cannot do any real work or assume any independence."[3] And Stella Jones, who herself has experienced the vagaries and vicissitudes of moving, found that 10 percent of the wives she surveyed in a study admitted unhappiness with changing homes. Moreover, she observes, "When they're unhappy, they're really unhappy." Yet the vast majority of the women were apparently willing to adjust to moving with their husbands' jobs "even if it causes them some pain."[4]

Women's Liberation has uncovered special hardships for skilled and professional women in regard to moving. There is the case of the professor whose wife is also an academician. She often cannot be employed at the same college or university because of a rule against nepotism. This prohibition generally penalizes the wife when the husband changes posts, especially if they move to a small community. The woman either remains unemployed or is forced to take a job at a lower level of teach-

ing, such as high school or junior college, when her training and quali-
fications equip her for higher-level performance. Although the nepotism
rule might work against the male, this is a rarity, for quite apparent
reasons. Many women have adjusted to such an inequity without apparent ill effects, but one wonders what this renunciation, coupled with
many others that women automatically make in society, ultimately
produces.

Happily most wives do not suffer the fate of the woman described
in the Prologue. The vast majority have made adjustments and adapta-
tions, displaying remarkable elasticity and resilience in difficult and trying circumstances. If excessive drinking or physical complaints do surface as defenses against insecurities and self-doubts, they are usually
contained within limits tolerable to others and to themselves. Possibly
the most noteworthy thing about corporate wives is not that some of
them develop illnesses when uprooted but rather that the vast majority
indeed retain the capacity to gain personal pleasure from the successes
of other persons (their husband and children) and do so with a great
deal of competence and grace. They are a hardy breed, who like most
human beings are fresh and eager at the outset but who understandably
and humanly wear down under what are often inordinate pressures.

The relatively few instances of serious breakdown, however, do not
negate the suffering that transfers place on countless corporate families.
As mentioned earlier, *The Wall Street Journal* article brought scores of
letters, many indicating instances of uprooting that I had not anticipated. In addition "Dear Mr. Success: Consider Your Wife" apparently
touched a sensitive nerve in diverse other areas. I was invited to appear
on the hour-long "Phil Donahue Show," a nationwide telecast originat-
ing from WLWV-TV in Dayton. The article was extensively quoted by
news columnist Paul Harvey both in print and on the air. The National
Association of Postal Supervisors reprinted it in the April 1972 issue
of its monthly magazine *The Postal Supervisor,* which is distributed to
36,000 members. The leadership of this organization had a special interest in the article, the magazine's editor wrote me, because "Postal Service officials are just about ready to upset tradition in the Postal Service
by putting into effect a mobility plan similar to industry for supervisors
and postmasters. There is much fear and apprehension among its members. I know that your article would be very interesting and
timely . . . and could even affect the thinking of Postal Service top
officials." Requests were similarly received and granted to reproduce
"Dear Mr. Success . . ." in two textbooks: *Readings in Sociology,* and
Sociology: A Text with Adapted Readings, by Dr. Leonard Broom and
Philip Selznick.

I sacrifice modesty in detailing these most gratifying responses with the intention of answering those who may see the impact of uprooting as episodic, idiosyncratic, or singularly pathological. The public reaction gives clear and confirming evidence that the problem is a general one and not the product of a neurotic or pampered mind. It is an existential one as well in that it results from a set of social and psychological circumstances to which we all may be heir, in company with the correspondents whose letters are quoted in the following pages.

Writing from Waltham, Massachusetts, to *The Wall Street Journal,* Diane Sorota O'Dwyer posed the problem eloquently:

The dilemma of Mr. Success' wife who increasingly must come to think of herself as "Mrs. Failure," a nonperson without credentials as Dr. Seidenberg describes her, is a national disgrace. Those who have for so long perpetrated the "unwritten" rules concerning appropriate behavior for the wives of successful and potentially successful men might do well to consider the tragic results they have engendered. Must it be axiomatic that a man's success in business be in inverse proportion to his success in his personal life? Are dysfunctional wives to continue to be a byproduct of corporate achievement and to present yet another pollution problem by wasting valuable human resources?[5]

Michael Fenton, of White Plains, New York, wrote sympathetically:

I believe that our large corporations would do well to apply the moral of this story to their own provincial practices of hopping managers and their families around the country (world) without regard to the traumatic effects on wives and children. Instability of family life, which includes the home location, certainly has its effects on the ability to perform. I've seen too many alcoholic wives, delinquent children, and misplaced souls in my life among the corporate movers. Perhaps someday our large corporations will consider the families of their employes when they "shoot old Joe off to Podunk to run the sheet-metal works down there."

This letter came from a woman living in a small town in Ohio:

I saw you on "The Phil Donahue Show" several weeks ago. I was very much interested in your comments about this mobile society. I have been married 2½ years, and we've lived in five different states ranging from Colorado to Pennsylvania. Three of the moves were with the army. . . . We moved to Ohio about four months ago, and a more unfriendly town I've never seen. No effort was made by my husband's employer to help us find housing or meet people. I've found the experience rather difficult. Since we will be moving again in a year, I wonder if you have any suggestions that would be helpful to a "family on the move."

And these are the words of a correspondent from Pittsburgh:

I am one of those [transferred] wives and run into many of them. We are a breed of our own, and there is much need of help and concern in the majority of the women. There are very few who take the moves without some devastating effect upon the mental health.

The following letter had no address and was signed "A Gypsy Wife":

I wonder if it is the loss of *status* which makes it so difficult for some of us. In my own case it is more the loss of *dear* friends, the kind that take years to make and that are not easily replaced. Bonding is a process which is somewhat limited, I should think. In my new location, I have been able to make many new friends, but the relationships are still somewhat superficial and constrained by the fact that most are wives of coworkers of my husband, which certainly makes confidences limited. This kind of superficial friendship does serve to pass the time pleasantly, but in time of crisis, is terribly inadequate.

Another difficulty is that in moving, the *only* seasoned relationships you take with you are [those] of the nuclear family. Perhaps most central is that of your husband, the reason you moved in the first place—to cleave unto him. If after this move, in which you have stripped yourself of the other old and true relationships, trouble arises with your husband, you are as alone as alone can be. In my case, my husband got involved with someone at the office. It's a recipe for collapse—in a marital crisis with no deep friends. The move makes you almost pathologically dependent on a single person; and inconstancy on the part of that person is devastating. In the old location, one is somewhat diversified in terms of relationships. Moving gives one person a monopoly; and that monopoly is dangerous.

I don't know what the solution is. Perhaps on our next move—this September—I'll try to move directly into a job, which will at least keep me from being so dependent upon my husband and preoccupied with him in a daily sense. But he will still be, because of the dynamics of moving, the emotional core, all others having been left behind once again. Certainly I never thought at age 34 to end up in a psychologist's office. But the *combination* of infidelity on the part of my husband with the loss of other relationships because of a move was devastating. The move seemed harmless as long as the marriage was not threatened. But threaten the marriage and the loss caused by moving becomes apparent. So your thoughts about the price of moving came at a sensitive time for me, and I thank you for them.

A suburban wife in New Jersey wrote thus:

Everything you said [on "The Phil Donahue Show"] was exactly as I have always maintained. On the East Coast this is a very common occurrence. As an R.N. [registered nurse] and mother of two children, I have met and known personally so many of these people of whom you speak.

14

Just three weeks ago I found myself in this same position. The move was to be to Chicago. I refused to go. I am no "shrinking violet" as some of those women on the show might think. I am 96 pounds of energy. My husband and I built our home with our own hands before we were married 22 years ago. We have constantly added to it over all these years. . . . I love my home and my life. I don't care if my husband never goes any higher. He is plant engineer of a large company (mechanical engineer), so he does better than I ever expected after living on a nurse's salary for years. I know that I would not get involved in Red Cross, church, PTA, and all those other organizations if I moved.

Many women that you described are right here in this little town. Alcohol and tranquilizers are the order of the day. It is too bad that this show could not be seen by our husbands. Mine will not believe me if I try to tell him each and every thing that was said. Our relationship is still strained over my refusal to move. I desperately need a copy of your article. If possible, could you please send me a copy and I will reimburse you. It sure would help to have it explained to him by someone other than myself.

The following letter was from a fashionable suburb of Cleveland:

This is my first "fan letter"; however, having seen and heard you on Phil Donahue's show today, I feel that I should voice my appreciation. I am not an executive's wife although my husband is an engineer in management. Our moves, 10 in 15 years, were to various cities and twice to New York City. They were not caused by transfers but rather for mergers, layoffs, or a step up in another company. During the first moves, I quickly made friends—then had to leave them. I am an extrovert and a college graduate so this was not difficult. However, each time I retreated, and finally I just quit bothering about the outside. Our final move was over four years ago back to Cleveland, where we had lived for 14 years before our trek. Then I had the nervous breakdown which had been in the making. I have been in the hospital five times since then, but now think I am on my way back because I again have found the faith that I will not have to move again. Learning this morning that there are many, many cases like mine helps to allay the belief that I was weak in character. For that I thank you.

A correspondent from Indiana said:

It came as a shock to learn I'm not alone in my feelings about moving. I have been thoroughly brainwashed to believe that "other women" move with complete ease and perfect adjustment. We recently moved here after spending nine years in a small community in California. In the 15 years of our marriage, we've moved over 2,000 miles eight different times. I always felt insecure, but it has become worse with the added responsibility of three children, 11 and 9 years and 18 months.

15

The last move was made against my wishes. But the only alternative was to divorce and try to raise three children successfully on my own. I'm not strong enough for this. Although I'm responsible for their development, I don't have the added worry of their material support. In California I had recently completed an L.P.N. course and was hoping to take night courses until my youngest is in school, then go on to become a registered nurse. I find nursing very satisfying. I had made several *close* friends and many acquaintances.

In the short time we have been here, I've gone downhill, almost to the bottom. My dear father passed away suddenly in January. I made a short heartbreaking trip back to California. Now I sit here in a messy house, with stringy hair, completely and totally unhappy. When the older children come home from school, I make an effort, or when the baby isn't napping, I devote my time to him. The rest of the time I sleep or stare at the television. How can this be happening to me? What am I doing to my family? I am not a weak person. I was always active and interested. What to do?

We went to a psychologist before making this move. He did not work on our marriage as such. My husband didn't have time to go back. I had testing and sessions. He told me I am sensitive and am depressed but no big problems. I became interested in working with his drug patients during my spare time. I've applied for part-time work at the local hospital, but so far no openings. The women I have met are friendly, but they have known one another since childhood, and I am considered an outsider. Just as I was forcing myself to begin to put down roots, my husband's boss told him he would be transferred to St. Louis immediately. We went to St. Louis over the weekend to look the area over. Monday morning we were told things have changed.

Now I sit in this lonely house with no desire to put down roots. It is too painful to be uprooted. We have no idea if we will be moving again. What do I do about this painful existence? I'm so tired (no organic cause). I realize you can't answer all of the letters you receive, but I want to thank you for your understanding of the problems many of us have.

The final communication to be quoted, from "An Air Force Wife" now in Oklahoma, is an essay-length description of the struggles of a person on the move to keep marriage, family, and soul together. She kindly gave permission to use it here and edited it for greater clarity as well as matters of privacy. Her letter explained:

The April 1 issue of the *National Observer* carried an excerpt from an article in *The Wall Street Journal* written by you. I was amazed to see my personal "crisis" described so accurately and succinctly. The accompanying pages are something I wrote out about six weeks ago in an attempt at "autotherapy"—casting myself as both the patient and the sympathetic listening therapist. I'm sending it with the thought that you may be interested in it as a case study which very well documents your point. (Nothing has been changed to bring it into closer agreement with what you wrote—you and I, quite independently, have said the same thing.)

And here is her enclosure:

I have begun to feel that I can't take one more move in the next four years without going into severe future shock. Think I've taken the seven moves in the last nine years pretty much in stride, but this eighth move may be the next-to-the-last straw. To add to the problem, we always know, months in advance, that we're going to be transferred again. We moved to Tulsa in July, found out in November that another move was coming up, and there are still 3½ months before we can go ahead and get it over with. In the meantime I worry about finding a house and neighborhood that will provide me with the sense of security and well-being I get from being in harmony with my surroundings; about finding a suitable school arrangement for a child with a perceptual handicap; and about all the other large and small details involved in relocating in an unknown place, which always entails a degree of stress. I seem to be getting deeper into a state of anxiety and depression, with periods of psychic pain and ensuing fatigue and loss of all drive. I wake myself up at night grinding my teeth, am sleeping tensely and fitfully, having threatening dreams, and waking up tired. Rapid transience is really getting to me.

I moved to Wichita in 1951—22 years old, full of youth, ambition, idealism, energy, and faith that my efforts toward a better society and a full personal life were worthwhile. I became deeply involved in all kinds of activities, made a place for myself, and found lots of friends: intelligent, imaginative, involved individuals. In my years there I came to know the community theater group, the Great Books group, the University faculty group and a lot of the students, the Unitarian group, the Reform Jewish group, the Beat group, the black community leaders, the white community leaders, the people in the media, a lot of lovable nobodies, and even the John Birchers. I managed to keep house (more or less) and take care of two small children, and to be up to my eyeballs in activities that made me feel I was where it's at. After I started working at the university and then was divorced and started taking classes to finish my B.A. in addition to working, there wasn't much time for organized activities, along with still keeping house and raising children. But I was already established and didn't become an isolate. Having a satisfying job, a few other activities, a good group of friends, and a lot of friendly acquaintances was enough—except that I did want to marry again if I could find a man who was mature, stable, directed, intelligent, lovable, and willing to take on a family.

And I found him. I was 33 when Mike and I were married; then he moved me and the children to Salina, and my years of isolation—of being out of things and out of touch with Real People—began. In the two years in Salina and Michigan, I was busy finishing the last few hours of under-graduate work, having a baby, and coping with her difficult infancy; so there wasn't much time to try to get into anything—and we were just "passing through" those places anyway.

The two years in Columbia, when the baby had become a toddler, were better. We were greeted immediately by a good group of Instant Friends on the M.U. faculty, without having to work at it. I didn't have anything there but purely social activities (and some warm friendships), but it was enough for the period of our stay and for the time and energy I had then, and a lot more than the two previous places had offered.

The next two years, in San Antonio, were stressful, with working half time, getting a master's degree, and having a preschool child, two fiercely rebelling teenagers, a husband who felt neglected, and not a single friend in the vicinity. By the time I had begun to glimpse some possibilities for community, we were about to be transferred again. The nine months in Japan were a restful change, and there were lots of fascinating things to see, but it was another period of social isolation and nonachievement. Last year in Wichita—while Mike was in Vietnam—was going home again after a long absence in a way; but knowing I'd be there only a year (and being tied down with a first-grader child, with no other family around), I didn't really settle in. Went back to work at the university and mostly spent evenings and weekends being a kind of halfhearted mother.

When we moved to Tulsa last summer, I was 42. With the prospect of being here for three years, I was ready to start doing the things necessary to end the state of being an uprooted isolate—though realizing that it gets harder as one gets older, somehow. Spent August fixing up the house, set aside September and half of October for surgery and recuperation, then emerged and found Tulsa to be a very open kind of place. Already I know some potential friends and am known fairly widely—am even on a committee for the city's Community Relations Commission, by invitation, and have ended up on the mailing list of every liberal organization in town.

But in November we were notified that the Tulsa office was being cut down, and another assignment was imminent. One month later orders for Dayton came through, with Mike to report there the end of February. Our daughter and I will stay in Tulsa until her school year ends, but I don't have much heart for pursuing activities or friendships here now. Am thinking about the prospect of starting all over again in another strange place—and I'm so tired! We're supposed to be in Dayton for four years (but then we were supposed to be in Tulsa for three years and it turned out to be six months for Mike). It takes about a year really to get into a new place and make some friends, so if I start right away, there could be about three years to enjoy the fruits of my efforts. If we're transferred again after a year or so, those efforts will have been in vain; but if I don't try and we're not transferred, it would mean another four years of isolation.

18

If I still enjoyed all the community activities as much as I did in my 20s, it would seem far less formidable—but at this stage they represent the onerous and time-consuming process that must be gone into again in order to get acquainted with a (temporary) community and the interesting people therein. If I were a "typical" air force wife, who liked the social activities of the military community, the moves would be easier; but I'm not. The busy work of ladies' clubs, either military or civilian, turns me all the way off, too. I want to be a part of a civilian community but don't really want to throw myself whole hog into fund raising for good causes, building or holding together an idealistic organization, working on political campaigns, correcting social ills and injustices, putting on plays, seeking knowledge, or anything else. These things are important in my value system, but they require a great deal more time and energy than I have to give and often more community identification than I am able to muster, and they end up conflicting with other values about family responsibility.

. . . Maybe it's necessary to have your sights set on building Utopia—"A man's reach should exceed his grasp"—in order to keep going when all you may really accomplish is adding a few grains of sand to the concrete that will put it together. If I were a long-time resident with years ahead to work, I might hope to do my share in adding enough sand to make the cement for one brick that will go into building the new society. But I only have enough time to begin to find out where the sandpile is; then off we go again. At this point I ask myself, why even bother to look for it? One tends to leave a place psychologically well in advance of actual physical departure, and that's what happens to me all the time.

I suspect that at least some if not most of the active people realize that their goals are too big and far off to be achieved directly but thoroughly enjoy the *process* of strategy planning in working toward them. My problem may be that I no longer enjoy the process. I've become cynical because progress moves at an imperceptible rate if at all—and then there's my family situation and my responsibility hangup.

Mike . . . knows very well how to work, but that's *it*. When he's not working, he's passive. Therefore any efforts to find a place for us in a new community must be made by me. Mike goes along with me in whatever I may drum up—it makes him happy to make *me* happy—but the only things he ever initiates are occasional spectator-type activities, and those he initiates principally to entertain me. He is much more cynical than I am about Causes, but he also isn't motivated to get into *non*-Cause activities that might be fun or interesting and might provide some avenues for involvement with real live people.

Besides, his passivity outside the work area means that his highest value is a comfortable domestic life. . . . Which is where my sense of responsibility comes in—he's a kind, thoughtful, affectionate, generous husband who would do anything he could to make me happy. He demands virtually nothing in return, and it seems the least I can do is to try to provide what makes him comfortable and content: affection, interested attention, and security in his home life. Obviously this is a matter of self-interest (and affection) as well as responsibility—whatever I give is what I will get in return.

I'm not good at that role, however. Am not all that well-organized, basically, am not really fascinated with the details of homemaking, and need quiet time when I don't feel pressured and can goof off or meditate or withdraw. . . . If I get involved in community activities, hoping to be a pleasanter and happier and more alive person than I am as an isolate, either the well-organized house goes to pot or I don't have any unpressured goof-off time or both. These days I find myself growing irascible under the least pressure, which may be a menopausal manifestation; and almost everything seems like pressure, short of complete withdrawal. Unfortunately the fetal position is not feasible.

There may be a sense of aimless drifting that eventually comes with noninvolvement; but for now I think I could fill my time well enough with odd bits of homemaking, puttering in things that interest me, and relationships with people—if only I *knew* some people. What would fill the bill would be some friends who had lively interests and would drop in frequently with stimulating conversation. It takes time to develop friendships like that, though.

One available out is getting a job. With a cleaning lady once a week and only three of us at home, I contribute very little to the family—and less if I'm running around doing committee work and sloughing off the few domestic responsibilities that I do have. One cannot genuinely believe in Women's Liberation and at the same time live as a kept woman or a nonutilitarian chattel maintained by her husband as another item of conspicuous consumption. To justify my existence and maintain self-respect, I need to be doing something of economic value to the family unit—either outside the house earning or inside the house keeping the home fires burning and dispensing with the cleaning lady. Of the two I prefer working because it offers opportunities for interest, achievement, recognition, and human contact.

Getting a job is far from a perfect solution, however. For one thing, because we are so transient, I get short-term, rather flunky jobs. For another it's harder to get into anything in my work field when I'm a stranger in town: most of my jobs have developed because something has come up that calls for social research, and someone who knew me and believed in my ability and good faith asked me to do it. Third, if I am working and trying to hold down the fort at home, there's no time and energy left over for anything else. I have on occasion worked with people who were already or became a part of one of my friend groups, but I have never developed a group of friends from a working situation. Some individual on-the-job friends, but nothing that has led to much of anything outside the office. So I really need to be free of a job schedule long enough to get some social bridges built in a new location before settling into working.

20

Fourth, there is our child. I can't just take off and do things without regard for her school schedule or babysitting arrangements. As an "only" child, she makes more demands on her parents for attention. As a learning disability case, she requires some additional attention as well as trips to the tutor, conferences with her teachers, periodic doctors' appointments, and the like. She also needs close monitoring because she's not well programmed. All this channels off some of the time and energy that otherwise would be available for doing or thinking about other things—and I still don't do as much with her as I should.

Altogether I have the feeling that too much of the burden for trying to stay alive (mentally and emotionally) is on my sloping shoulders and that I'm on a treadmill that moves backward faster than I can make forward progress. I cringe at the prospect of more years ahead as an isolate—yet feel like collapsing at the thought of taking on another round of trying to break into another new community (for a few years only) and meanwhile trying to see to the needs of my family, domestic responsibilities, and working.

There doesn't seem to be any good solution for any of it. As long as Mike has enough to do at work to pass the time and has domestic comfort, he seems content to vegetate and spend the rest of his life waiting to die. It doesn't seem likely that he's going to loosen up and develop new drives toward anything but working. Our child's problems are not going to vanish into thin air. I can either keep struggling and muddling through poorly on all fronts, starting all over again every time we move—or I can quit fighting it and vegetate too. Wotthehell. For years I told myself that it would be different in the *next* place we lived, after we were out from under whatever stress currently had us tied down and when we could settle in a place for a few years. But now I've begun to think 'twill ever be thus.

Meanwhile I grow older, achier, tireder, more discouraged, and less ambitious. In a few years I'll probably give up, settle back, and grow solid mildew between my ears and where my guts once were. The only thing I'll worry about is trying to get our daughter through high school and married off to a nice boy who will take care of her. When that's done I can have my prefrontal lobotomy and be happy—or something. In a nutshell all the faith and enthusiasm necessary for keeping on trying to stay alive has been discouraged out of me. But the idea of spending the rest of my years just going through motions and coping with details and being not alive is grim and even terrifying. (Wallowing in self-pity may be good catharsis if not carried *too* far.)

Some of this is premove anxiety; I'm facing the unknown again and at this point wish we'd hurry up and move so I could get on about the business of locating doctors, dentist, the nearest grocery store, and where to shop for what, and then go through the period of meeting all the new strangers and hoping to find one or two who might be friends. Once that is done I'll probably feel a little better—unless, that is, we have been notified by that time that another transfer is coming up. If that happens I may just retreat permanently from whatever passes for reality.

These letters, like so many others that I have received, poignantly describe how it feels to be dragged away from friends and familiar surroundings without regard to one's own needs and aspirations as a person. Each of the women has dutifully gone along, realizing the struggles and anxieties that her husband is suffering, doing everything in her power to cooperate and lessen the burdens on him. Then the moment of truth comes in the third to fifth decade of her life—namely, the loss of self. And there is the bleak realization that little was done by anyone to lessen her burdens. Everyone has been kind in the new locales. Everyone has been dutiful. There have been the Welcome Wagons. Next-door neighbors have brought in cakes. All the form has been attended to meticulously. But how much inclination can a woman have to "settle in," as the air force wife put it, when she knows she may be unsettled within a few months?

There have of course been demurring responses to *The Wall Street Journal* essay and the points made on the television show. Some came from women: a 45-year-old telephone caller during the TV program who has moved to five states in nine years told us, "I don't mind moving at all." Some came from men: a letter reprinted in Chapter 5 points out how much strain transfers place on the husbands themselves.

But the overwhelming balance of the responses—from both men and women—confirm the feelings of loneliness and helplessness that women develop over time from having little or no say in their destinies. Readers and viewers understood, perhaps for the first time, that theirs is a very real, ubiquitous problem resulting not from their own inadequacies but from those of a system that denies them the conditions requisite for independent growth.

Women, an increasing number of corporate wives among them, are seeking employment not necessarily to supplement family income but to gain a sense of accomplishment. They, like their husbands, must have evidence of achievement outside the home to feel fully human. They are going into the professions when possible and opening their own businesses and enterprises. They are returning to schools and colleges to complete previously abandoned programs and to seek additional degrees. For these self-enhancing activities, one has to stay put.

The more a woman's identity becomes merged with a professional or business role of her own, the more resistance she will have to any move suggested by a husband or his company. In some instances she can make the move without loss; her own credentials may be transferable. But too often they are not, complicated as they may be by tenure at a college, points, seniority at a school or hospital, or the dependence of a business on favorable location as well as a built-up clientele.

Take the instance of the woman, married for 15 years and the mother of two children, who had established her own dancing school and had become known beyond her community for her skills and capabilities. Her husband was asked to move by the insurance company for which he was working. He was now needed in the home office, a promotion of considerable size. This was fine for him and for his family as well. Was the wife now expected to give up her dance studio and 75 students to start all over again in a distant community? To save her marriage and family, she did it, with the hope of starting up a similar school in the new city.

She made the move, but the new place already had what she could offer; there was no need for her specialized talents. She tried for five years to reestablish herself but with little success or reward. She thereupon left her husband (her children were now grown and away at schools) to resume her art in an area where there was acceptance of her talents. She was of course roundly condemned by some friends and family as a very selfish person.

But there will be an increasing number of such "selfish" women as they seek self-fulfillment in worldly terms and dimensions. There will be much condemnation and character assassination until there is genuine acceptance of women as full people with viable egos of their own. Moves will become more difficult and will place greater pressures on marriages. There are already some 33 million women in the workforce, of whom between 2 and 3 million are sole supports of families. The past stereotype of what a family is—husband as breadwinner and leader and wife as helpmate and follower—is fast fading. The concept of the sanctity of marriage is taking it on the chin. Traditional marriage is already under siege in America, with one out of three unions ending in divorce (one out of two in California).

Up until now we have tried to explain these statistics and upheavals as cases of individual "sickness," "immaturity," or "selfishness." This type of name calling will no longer serve to deal with basic inequities and mythologies in our social structure. Our world has changed beneath our feet—past palliatives and platitudes suffice no more.

WHY O WHY DID I
EVER LEAVE BIG SKY?

> *A person who* receives *nothing from his*
> *community loses an important stimulus*
> *of his humanity, and so does a person*
> *unable to* contribute *to his fellow citizens.*
> LIONEL TIGER and ROBIN FOX

THE CASE HISTORY in the Prologue seems a mild one, with but two moves, in comparison with the sagas of others who have moved as much as 20 times in the course of 15 years of marriage! Yet credentials are forfeited with each move, whether it is the first or the twenty-first; and depending on the character of the new locale, they may be lost from one section of a city to another. A woman who telephoned during "The Phil Donahue Show" reported that her family had moved a mile and a half, into a new church parish, and that two years had gone by before she had been able to find volunteer work—a principal activity in her life—with the new congregation. The diminution of influence in one's community is a hidden cost to the spirit, whatever the number or distance of moves.

The problem of losing credentials surely is not confined to the female or wife. Over the years I have seen severe reactions in men who have similarly been unable to transfer their credentials. I recall a Hungarian star soccer player who came to this country after the 1956 abortive revolution. A luminary in his enslaved country, he was a nobody in free America. At that time soccer players were not being used as place kickers in football. "Freedom" proved insufficient. There was no place for him in America other than as an ordinary person. He became emotionally disturbed and was hospitalized.

Many refugees must feel the same way but perhaps are too embarrassed to reveal their inner despair about such loss. This has very little to do with neurosis. Thankfully, during times of abundance, most refugees with skills and training are—with great effort to be sure—able to transfer their credentials and again achieve status. The age of the person obviously has a lot to do with his or her success, one in the 20s or 30s having a distinct time advantage. In *The War Lover* John Hersey described a similar phenomenon in the case of the American who was a "star" in war and in peacetime could not match the tremendous status and prestige of being an air force hero. Thus men are not exempt from the vagaries of loss and displacement.

There are people who spend their lives on the move and who claim to thrive on it. For these families the matter of transferring credentials is hardly an issue; theirs is a gypsy existence in which neither physical nor emotional unpacking is possible. Perhaps they can see themselves as citizens of the world, for their type of life militates against any significant community dimension. They can have little say in determining their own destinies and the future of the community they find themselves in at a given moment. Gypsies and nomads are romantic and beautiful people, but history is clearly against them; those who merely pitch tents have left little mark on civilization. They do not build churches, universities, libraries, and hospitals. To create these one has to be rooted and identified with an area as one's own. And as we will see shortly, it takes years to become established and to gain the power to build. The itinerant or transient must forgo the pride of such spirit-enhancing accomplishments and must remain a passenger, a recipient. What such nomadism ultimately does to the human spirit can only be surmised. Little wonder that the letter writers quoted in Chapter 1 felt such despair when forced into yet another transfer. They knew that their accomplishments would not carry the credentials they would need to be an effective force in the new community.

People do survive a dozen or more moves—a tribute to their iron will and determination—but the cost in withering and alienation may be staggering. Biologically the human organism can withstand a great deal, as our space probers have clearly demonstrated. However, it is often the exercising of societal and community prerogatives, which involve power, status, and authority, that changes *existing* into *living*. This dimension of personhood is often lost when one is on the move. A person or family is thereby diminished and may suffer, as the philosophers would say, a teleological death. To exert a meaningful influence on a community, one generally must have roots in it, often several generations of involvement. It is not just a matter of having money; one cannot easily buy oneself into the inner circles. Old money generally prevails over new.

A top executive learned this in a city in upstate New York. There some 15 years as head of a large corporation employing several thousand people, he embarked on a community project of establishing a new general hospital, for which there was a great need. With characteristic efficiency he formed a committee and an organization to promote this effort. Never failing in any business project he sponsored, he had high confidence in this enterprise. His whole training had been geared to selling new products to the populace.

From the tone of this description, the reader is correct in surmising that he failed completely. After 18 months of arduous work, the committee was dissolved. The hospital was eventually built but by other and "older" hands. He had erred grievously in assuming that his good intentions and noble motives could supersede or transcend the established means and avenues of getting things done in that community. He neglected to investigate the root structure of the city, with its intertwining tentacles that controlled the significant levers of power. Without this knowledge and adequate cultivation of these persons, he could do nothing. There was no substitute for the root system. They resented his intrusion and what they considered his arrogance. He was a newcomer even after 15 years and a record of devotion to the community.

This defeat had a devastating effect on him from which he never fully recovered. Although his corporation continued to prosper under his direction, he never again extended himself into public or community life. Gradually he and his family transferred their interests to a city with a "warmer" climate.

How long does it take to establish bona fide credentials in such a community, credentials strong enough to enable one to make significant changes? One response is: three generations. Perhaps this is a cynical exaggeration, but it is not too far from the truth. Many newcomers never realize their societal impotence because they half-intentionally avoid the type of confrontation that this executive attempted. People like to think that what they don't know won't hurt them.

The community, because of its chauvinism and xenophobia, lost the services of a valuable citizen. It was to its discredit that the entrenched majority did not extend helping and welcoming hands to an adopted member. But these are the existential realities of life; two Americas are evolving 60-40, the entrenched and the mobile.

On the other hand fairness requires us to ponder whether some community resistance to newcomers may be due to the attitudes of the incoming residents themselves. Certainly there are people who say to themselves, if we are going to be here a short time only, why worry about (or vote for) sewer construction, improvement of schools, and health facilities? This leads to an erosion of local interest and participation so that both power and decisions revert to the more distant state and federal agencies. In fact Vance Packard, in *A Nation of Strangers,* attributes much of community anarchy and neglect to the indifference of the mobile section to local problems. He feels that "Increasing rootlessness of people . . . has a lot to do with what ails America as a society."[1]

Thus because of entrenched community suspicions and the indifference of those on the move, communities lose the resources and services of a large number of highly educated, talented people; and these same people are deprived of the exercise of a dimension of human experience, a loss that must leave them with a sense of frustration leading to a special loneliness and alienation.

Should a husband expect his wife—or himself for that matter—to stick it out in a hostile community? To be able to adjust to an inhospitable environment may appear a most desirable attribute from his employer's standpoint, but it may also indicate a lack of character, conviction, and pride. William H. Whyte, in his essay "The Wife Problem," has a good word to say about the "ornery" wife who won't adapt:

> "Adapt" is a meaningless word unless it is considered in relation to what one is supposed to be adapting to. . . . To illustrate: there are a good many case histories at hand in which the husband has given up a job at a new post because his wife did not take to the community. Was she wrong? In the new lexicon of values, yes; as the obeisance paid "adapt" indicates, it is the environment that should be the constant; the individual, the variable. But might not she have been right after all? Some towns *are* stifling and backward, and one can adapt to them only by demeaning oneself. Should she, then, adapt? And if so, why?[2]

Journalist George Vecsey writes of Dean and Stella Jones, "Dr. Jones took a job with the University of Utah at Salt Lake City, and they felt for the first time 'what it was like to be part of a minority group in America.' "[3] They did not experience any prejudice there—just the massive pervasiveness of the Mormon Church, which seemed to extend into all areas of life. After two weeks Dr. Jones felt that Salt Lake City was not the place for him, and his wife agreed. Mrs. Jones felt that she had moved into an entirely different culture, engendering the specter of things being "beyond my control—yet I was confronted by them."

Pressure for conversion can be enormous and overwhelming in a community with a particularist population. Those who want to establish businesses and professions often find that the only way to survive in it is to adopt the residents' faith. For families who have moved to it

27

because of the husband's transfer to a national concern or government installation, the principal burden and hardship fall on the wife and children. The husband is accepted at work because of his skill and credentials as an executive or professional man. On the other hand the wife must fight her way into a generally hostile community. I am told that outsider wives meet together where they console and comfort one another in group psychotherapy fashion.

Probably Mormons are no more biased or chauvinistic than other groups in America. They themselves were the objects of discrimination, ridicule, and exploitations in their early days. It is a regrettable fact of life that victims, who have suffered themselves, often apply a reverse golden rule to newcomers: do unto others what has been done unto you.

This is a sad consequence of the brutalization process that repeats itself when the powerless become the powerful. In psychoanalytic terms, it is known as identification with the aggressor. Somehow, having been victims of oppression, we imitate our oppressors the first chance we get. Can the cycle be broken? Perhaps nonadherents to the established faith in particularist communities may know how Jews might feel in a rural area that knew of them only for "what they did to Christ"—or how black people feel most anywhere outside their enclaves.

After reading my article in *The Wall Street Journal,* a woman with a similar experience wrote to me expressing her outrage. She was horrified at suddenly finding herself an alien and a member of a minority group in her own country! To feel thus abroad is one thing, but for a Methodist to be considered *un*-Christian in Protestant America defies endurance and toleration. And she is right. A human being with conviction and passion should not be expected to adjust to such an environment. The Joneses fled immediately. My correspondent, because of age and other circumstances, could not. Her indignation was proper and healthy. Thankfully she is able to articulate her frustrations and fury. Others, sadly, may blame themselves for "not being able to adjust." Here the "ornery wife" clearly is the healthy one.

The French sociologist Emil Durkheim diagnosed the condition of the individual resulting from such a loss of traditional community supports as *anomie. Anomie* is literally a feeling of disorientation, a not knowing exactly who you are or where you are in time and place. Durkheim felt that it was the sense of common purpose and togetherness mainly in the social areas of existence that facilitated orientation. With uprooting these facilities all but disappear unless other organizations such as corporations provide adequate substitutes.

Whyte describes the substitution of the corporation for the community that comes about inadvertently and negatively when transfers

28

preclude integration into the general populace. For those who move a great deal, so that they never have the time or the energy to take root or make friends, the corporation for good or bad becomes the main interest. In such instances a family never really unpacks and may look forward to the next move as an adventure, albeit in a closed and sheltered system. The superficial sameness of the various locations, a sort of countrywide uniformity of physical surroundings that Chapter 3 will describe briefly, still does not allow vital relationships to develop. Richard Reeves writes:

> The corporate families are the interchangeable solid citizens of an endless suburb—when an office manager at Allied Chemical in Wayne, New Jersey, is transferred, his house is filled by a new district sales manager for Dayton Rubber whose old house in Clayton, Missouri, is filled by an engineer at General Dynamics. The suburbs, I suspect, have become a kind of decentralized national company town. The vital coin of the national company town has to be small talk because in the end the people next door never really know each other—they only know they are the same.[4]

For the wife who moves frequently, the sun never sets on company soil, and whether out of renunciation or resignation, she puts her fate in with that of the corporation. She may then become fiercely loyal to it, as one would to one's family. Going to a different seat of the corporation empire becomes a welcome test of adaptability and "kind of a vacation sometimes." Whyte observes, "Because moving makes their other roots so shallow and transitory, the couple instinctively clings all the harder to the corporation." There is a hidden price for all of this. Even when the company-integrated couples turn uprooting into a virtue, they express apprehension about what it does to children, a subject that Chapter 4 will detail. But for themselves, having abrogated autonomous living, the company comes to stand *in loco parentis*. Then what otherwise might be considered intrusions on independence and invasions of privacy become benefits and rewards. Thus one wife explained, "Eastman Kodak has wonderful good-will policies; I used to have to attend to all the home details like insurance and bills. Now the company has someone who does these things for you—they even plan vacations for you."[5] Whyte comments that these wives look upon the company as a beneficent Big Brother. One might ask, does such help strengthen or weaken a person?

The natural disorientation of living in a foreign country inclines families sent overseas to turn even more to the corporation as a community substitute. The American multinational companies, those with branches spread throughout the world, are often more powerful than the countries in which they do business. It is known for instance that General Motors, with annual sales in 1972 amounting to more than $30 billion, exceeded the individual gross national product of all but some 15 countries of the world. Critics see these giant corporations as private states that place their own interests above the countries they reside in. The virtues or detrimental effects of this development are not directly our concern. However, the size and power of such worldwide organizations do have effects on the community feeling of employees and their families. In many instances loyalty to the company transcends allegiance even to their nation. Families proudly identify with the corporation, and moves for it are often viewed almost patriotically as assignments for the mother country.

In this context, if one does not look too deeply into problems of exploitation or corporate imperialism, employees and their families can derive tremendous pride from working for a company on whose branches the sun never sets. In addition there is emotional security in the feeling that they are never very far from a company resource. The effect of seeing the company's emblem in far-off places may be compared with the thrill President Nixon reported on seeing the American flag flying from the Kremlin during his 1972 trip to the Soviet Union. Sentimental hogwash, the cynic may retort, but all the same, who among us is so well integrated of mind, body and soul that he can do without the security that identification with power brings? This power along with its symbols helps dispel loneliness and despair. For the employee and his family, torn from their native land, the multinational company becomes a community within which needs are met, security gained, and credentials developed at almost any level. Hence families traveling or transferred from country to country cultivate corporation people as their friends and learn to depend on corporation facilities and resources as their objects of belonging.

For the corporate wife serving abroad, integration into the multinational corporation means that her job, in addition to managing the household and her children, is to entertain indigenous company bigwigs and traveling executives. If she is in one place for any length of time, she gains longevity status, as do members of the diplomatic corps. This entails responsibilities for helping and instructing corporation newcomers in their new homes. She also earns deference from newly arrived wives of company men. As they too integrate into the company, matters of social life and entertaining as well as dress and manners come under her scrutiny. All become engaged in the work of promoting and augmenting company image and prestige.

Personal interests or activities apart from the corporation are strictly no-nos in a foreign land, where possible involvements with host-country enterprises are always subject to controversy, misinterpretation, or both. So there is virtually no alternative to company integration for the corporate wife except visiting museums (if there are any) or crawling the walls. Self-abnegation is almost complete; hopefully the rewards and compensations that accrue from husband and corporation are enough to balance the loss of personal identity and private amibitions. Many make it; others give the appearance of making it.

But living in an enclave, separated and alienated from all but other employee families and their servants, eventually wears down the soul. A person's humanity diminishes under such conditions of actual and spiritual segregation. As the need for free participation in a social or political community is thwarted, atrophy inevitably sets in. Women in such circumstance over a period of years actually welcome the dependence and protection of the corporation. The development of this devotion and loyalty is generally interpreted as a favorable turn of events. Isn't this a most desirable result—getting two "cooperative" people for the price of one? But in reality it is submission out of desperation; someone may have died in the process.

Military wives, subjected as they are to their husband's many moves and long absences, share the destiny of their civilian counterparts. Yet in many ways they are better off than their corporate sisters. True, the financial and material rewards may not be so great, but for obvious reasons the service wife has greater preparation for what is to come. Moreover a greater protective spirit appears to work in her behalf. Nancy Shea informs us that there are hospitality committees at each air force base to help newcomers out, and a system of "spotters" has been developed whereby incoming wives are routinely visited and "rescued."[6]

There is also a structure to military living that can be quite reassuring. Families more or less know what to expect. Each post is not too different from the next, and it provides a built-in community to which they can readily adjust, though this may—and usually does—entail ignoring the surrounding environment. For better or worse social life is highly structured, and credentials (the husband's rank) are transferable from one post to another.

The inbreeding of such circumscribed forms of community life, however, can regrettably promote artificial values. This is commonly the case with corporate families living overseas—usually in enclaves—in countries with standards of living far below the level that American salaries reach. A colonialist mentality, growing out of the concept of

31

a private state, comes to permeate both the relationships in the family and its members' attitudes toward others.

Within the family itself the father, after 10 or 15 years of being a master over "native" workers to a degree that subordinates back home would not accept, can see no reason why his wife and children should not similarly submit to his superiority. The wife and children likewise feel themselves superior to the host population, present in their lives mainly as servants or suppliers of goods. In various ways the family's status is elevated by dint of its affiliation with the corporation well beyond the stratum it occupies on its own hearth.

The day of reckoning comes when the employee and his family are pitted against their "equals" at home, where their former special advantage no longer holds. Children get their comeuppance when they must compete with fellow American students who have only minimally inflated ideas about them. Similarly the father has a hard time when he returns. He will find his feelings of importance challenged not only by independent-minded staff members at work but by service people at every filling station and restaurant. He will be appalled by the high taxes and poor police protection, and he will be outraged by the permissive attitudes in our schools. His wife, accustomed to commanding a staff of servants abroad (however lazy and inefficient), will have to be contented with a cleaning woman twice a week who costs what she paid two live-in girls abroad. This diminution in status often leads to personal bewilderment and frustration.

Many corporate Americans who have lived abroad have made themselves a make-believe world, with a resultant distortion of their egos—a distortion not easily rectified. This is the unseen price that colonialists have always paid. The damage to one's own reality-testing ability is as bad as any purported exploitation of "natives." For the corporate American overseas, this has been his principal occupational hazard.

The human spirit thus needs a community in which character may grow, not wither—one that reinforces a person's grip on reality, not loosens it. The verity that humans are social animals implies scope and freedom of association. We do not do well when forced into ghettos.

Some readers may say that community influence or gratification of any breadth is a luxury of elitists, that most people live their lives totally absorbed in their families and direct their energies toward gaining economic security. A family lives where the man can make a living, they say. True, first things first. But just as an infant can actually die if only its physical requirements are attended to, with its need for contact left unfilled, so an adult can disintegrate when deprived of significant community ties. In a light vein we have all heard about people hustled

32

through Europe on bargain tours orienting themselves with "It's Tuesday; this must be Belgium!" But the disorientation that takes place as a result of continuous uprooting is often no joke.

One corporate wife, after a series of moves in the seven years of her marriage, sought help because she was literally having difficulty with time, dates, and appointments. She found herself missing social engagements, doctors' appointments for herself and her children, and most distressing of all the birthdays of her children! When the last happened she became acutely frightened—this was an unforgiveable lapse for any mother, she felt. She wondered if she was falling apart, and if so, why?

In the initial interview she indicated that she loved her husband and was happily married. Similarly she loved the new location and was making friends easily. She felt no resentment about the many moves the family had made. She would never consider opposing any move that her husband deemed necessary. As a matter of fact, after 18 months he was already complaining about this area as lacking in facilities and challenge and was toying with the idea of still another move. And, she insisted, she would happily move again if he made such a decision.

During the session she kept looking at her watch. What happened to the time? About another appointment next week, she couldn't think that far ahead. She would have to call back. Would I write down for her my fee and the length of the sessions? She would not be able to remember them to instruct her husband.

This from an intelligent woman with advanced college degrees who had lost control of her own destiny and with it her sense of time and place. Because of pride and loyalty, she doggedly denied the pain and anxiety she was experiencing from the merciless uprooting to which she had been subjected. Everything was wonderful and joyful, but she must get help so that she would not forget a child's birthday again! It is so characteristic of these soul-damaged women not to connect their *anomie* to what has been done to them but instead blame themselves for not being able to be perfect wives and mothers.

It is through just such a mechanism of denial that newcomers to a community are able to bear the pain of being excluded from full citizenship. They say, "Who cares?" or "I wouldn't want all that trouble" or "Those things are of no concern to us." These people are, however, diminished in spirit beyond what shows or what is admitted. For the ancient Greeks there was no crueler punishment than to be banished from the locus and functions of the "city," that is, the community. There was nothing worse than ostracization—nothing more degrading than to lose one's influence.

And there is the matter of friends. We all know the old saw: you inherit your relatives, but you can choose your friends. Friends indeed have a special value because we can choose them and because they in turn choose us. In this we become very special, select people. Here people come together because there is a sincere mutual attraction, strictly voluntary. There are no blood ties or binding laws, moral and legal, as in family relations and marriage. Having to give up or be separated from friends is a major trauma of moving, especially for wives and children. Men have their work and the sometimes too numerous associates derived from it. And because men travel a great deal in the course of business, they are more easily able to renew past friendships and acquaintances. Yet even among men, who are not "permitted" to be sentimental about such matters, separations from good friends, habitual golf partners, or familiar poker players are hidden sorrows.

It takes time to make new friends and to break into established circles. Adults moving into a new area maintain a reserve about themselves, an aloofness that belies the anxiety of wondering whether one will ever fit in. One doesn't want to impose or intrude, and here there emerges the issue of pride: "We are no social beggars." Most often the social contacts are made through children—a Girl Scout troop or a Little League baseball team. Common interest in children's activities breaks down the timidities that keep the adults apart. Yet these are social contacts that may or may not grow into the friendships one knew before. It takes time for the trust to develop between people that permits the intimacies and confidences that make friendships so valuable—so human. "If I just had someone to talk to" is the universal lament of the uprooted. Having "someone to talk to" in the full meaning of the phrase is not a whimsical luxury but a need as strong as an instinct. People who do have "someone to talk to," a friend who will listen and who in turn will relate, put psychiatrists out of business. And ironically enough such consolation as a friend can give is rarely found in a husband, a mother, or a child. Blood is thicker than water, we are told; we might add that it is often too thick for comfort. A good friend on the other hand is just right. Women especially have need for a confidante. This is primarily because women are trained to live in the affective domain, and they need reassurances (often from other women) that they are handling their male-female relationships "properly." On the other hand men often cannot have a confidant, for they are taught to control their feelings, to not have emotions, to not admit to weakness. Thus whereas women readily seek an ear, a shoulder to cry on, men often panic when they are placed in a relationship where they actually feel relaxed, with the barriers let down.

Besides the matter of friends, there is the subtler and often unspoken issue of constituency. This term is generally thought of as a political one and not applicable to ordinary human beings. Not true. It does apply: we all build up a coterie of friends and acquaintances as well as colleagues whom we may call upon for special activities such as charity drives and school functions. At the same time we serve as constituents of others in mutually advantageous social and communal endeavors. This often temporary and loosely knit arrangement is a most important source of clout in promoting some community or personal endeavor, like calling Minutemen of the American Revolution together for the national purpose: the urgent gathering of blood donors in the case of a family medical emergency for example. It is most comforting to have a constituency beyond confidants or friends when there is a pressing need for numbers.

The previous pages have pointed out some of the reasons behind the profound human need for community. There is another, known in both psychiatry and sociology, and perhaps lying close to the heart of the matter. It is expressed at the end of this excerpt from an article in *Life* magazine that is incidentally most germane to the issues of identity, transfer of credentials, and uprooting:

> In the past 70 years all the social forces surrounding marriage have drastically changed. When America was essentially rural and people stayed put, the values and voices of Lynn's larger family would have enveloped and supported her. And there was not the concern then about identity. On the farm the family was more of a team, working together on almost every aspect of living and survival, including education and religion.
>
> But now, Lynn's marriage existed in an urban, anonymous mobile world. And today, aside from child-rearing, the prime job of marriage is to provide emotional contact. Isolated in their shifting, rootless world, the members of the nuclear family—mother, father and children—are asked to answer every emotional need for each other. As a result the family often turns in upon itself, and the members consume each other.[7]

". . . The members consume each other" often because of the lack of interaction with the outside community. The pressure on the family unit becomes too great for any of its members to bear. The circuit becomes overloaded and explodes. Therefore it is vital that the members of the family have resources for gratification beyond one another. All too often the nuclear family must serve as an emotional supermarket where all things are supposed to be found—and also devoured. It is the deprivation of community consequent on uprooting that we are exploring. Thus diminished below a sustaining level, family members frequently turn on each other.

An extreme manifestation of this grueling state of affairs is the national statistic that most crimes of violence in America are committed in the home, against members of one's own household, not on the street. This fact bespeaks constricted, isolated living that gives family members little or no constructive outlet for pent-up energies. It is ironic indeed that we always hurt the ones we "love." The individuals involved in these instances of family discord and violence have little or no knowledge of the social and psychological forces that enfeeble and frustrate them. Feeling horribly deprived and put upon, they mistakenly see their own kin as oppressors and villains. They are unable to understand that their agonies stem from their own incapabilities as well as the partial or total absence of opportunities for gratifying their personal needs in the social environment.

Sadly, an overbearing and possessive man or woman may demand that all the family's pleasures come through one of them. He or she may bitterly resent the mate or child who shows independence of spirit by turning to outsiders and outside activities for fulfillment and enrichment. Here a husband gets violently jealous when his wife is seen talking to another man. There a mother is deeply wounded when her daughter spends time with a woman down the street, having found an adult friend of her own. Instead of being proud of the child's resourcefulness, the mother becomes petulant and petty: "After all I do for you, you prefer to be with a complete stranger!" The mother is probably envious of her child's ability to be free with other people, an ability the mother herself has lost in the alienating uprooting process.

Wives of public figures know the tremendous strains that mobility imposes. News commentator Paul Harvey, responding to my *Wall Street Journal* article, writes: "That success is a merciless marriage-wrecker should be acknowledged and understood before the fact." He quotes the wife of California's governor, Nancy Reagan, who says that the "only way for a governor's wife to keep from feeling sorry for herself is to concentrate very hard on the advantages." Also, Ruth Graham, wife of evangelist Billy Graham, "resigns herself to his preoccupation by constantly remaining mindful of the ordination and the importance of his work." Then Harvey wonders whether witnessing the tragic cost of rootlessness to high-achievement families "has disenchanted a whole generation of young people with the success syndrome."[8]

Judy Harkison writes specifically of the plight of political wives,[9] noting that the strain of political life with campaigning "has taken its toll as evidenced by the spate of Congressional separations and divorces—Representative Paul N. McCloskey, Jr., of California (separated); Senator John V. Tunney of California (divorce suit filed); Senator Robert J. Dole of Kansas (divorced); and Senator Proxmire [of Wisconsin] (separated)." And to this is added the public uncoupling of the John Mitchells, with Martha announcing that she was leaving her husband until he decided to leave his job as President Nixon's campaign manager.

Wives of political figures most often become integrated into their husbands' careers and campaigning. Muriel Humphrey's integration apparently has been quite successful. Through the strenuous campaigning, with parades, speaking engagements, visits to hospitals, and myriad other activities, her enthusiasm has remained undaunted; to her it is "a wonderful experience."

But for other wives of men in politics, the life often has less than salutary effects on the marriage and home life. Ellen Proxmire is quoted as saying: "Politics has a way of becoming all-pervasive. This is where I drifted away. I didn't want to be involved 100 percent of the time in the office or in a campaign or in someone else's campaign. All of a sudden you can find yourself locked into this with no outside interests and outlets and no time to develop anything else." The effects on children are similarly doleful. She tells of their 10-year-old son's prayer at dinner: "Thank you for having us all together for dinner this time. Take care of Dad on his trip tomorrow—and, by the way, [Dad,] where did you say you were going this time?"

An unintegrated political wife is Betty Talmadge, wife of Georgia's senator. She neither shares her husband's interest in politics nor takes an active part in his campaign. Instead she has run a meat business of her own since 1951, with annual sales of $3.5 million. She has raised her children in what appears to be a successful marriage and healthy family life, freely admitting that she rarely sees her husband! They each have separate careers that fill their lives, caring for their own growth and fulfillment. Neither makes inordinate sacrifices for the other.

Are they on to something?

STAY AND DECAY

Americans are always moving on. . . .
"We don't know where we're going, but
we're on our way!"
STEPHEN VINCENT BENET

THE POET TELLS US that "Americans are always moving on," a romantic image in the abstract—often a source of great damage concretely. But this does not mean that movement is an evil, to be avoided at all costs; one must remember that America grew strong on the mobility of its people.

We have always valued both social and geographic mobility. When Horace Greeley said, "Go west, young man," America was in need of muscle power and brain power all across the country. If opportunity was good in the East, the challenge and rewards might be even greater in the West.

The waves of immigrants from Europe and Asia were people on the move who had suffered and absorbed the pain of uprooting for the opportunity to make a living and enjoy certain freedoms unknown in the countries they left behind. America then comes from moving stock—men and women who left their entrenched, rooted kin behind. Although America never did become the melting pot envisaged by some, the constant churning and circulating did mold a country with a remarkable unity despite acknowledged racial and other social divisions. A strong industrial nation had a seemingly endless need for people.

By the mid-twentieth century, even the gas stations had taken on a national uniformity that makes people feel that America is one big home town. Children on the move can have the same flavor of ice cream at the Howard Johnson restaurant 3,000 miles from home. Even the rest rooms look the same coast to coast. All superficial technicalities, to be sure, and to the cynics proof of the banality of American life; but if not real friendliness, they at least exude an image of friendliness and some of the comfort derived from familiarity.

The freedom to move was encouraged and enhanced by the constitutional prohibition against barriers to interstate commerce. Despite sectionalism people can go to remote parts of the land and find their own church, down to a particular denomination. National organizations of businessmen, chambers of commerce, scouting organizations, and fraternal orders all allow some transferability of credentials that makes people feel somewhat at home.

Our interstate highway and air travel systems are the most extensive in the world. And the ubiquitous automobile, now with trailer attachments, has become a mobile motel for adults as well as children. You don't really have to leave home—you can take it with you.

Some 40 million of us move each year; 12 million American families moved in 1972, spending close to $2 billion doing it. Nearly 2 million families move across state lines. California leads the nation in the number of families that move in and out of the state. This movement increases with prosperity; it is curtailed in recessions.

If we lose power in moving, we can lose status in being planted. In certain circles it is an embarrassment to work and mature in the town in which one was born. During the last century our cities were fed by the talents of the farms and small towns. People of creativity and imagination always moved toward areas of challenge and opportunity. The last few decades have seen the urban areas cluttered by masses of people seeking refuge from rural poverty and unemployment, in many instances due to farm mechanization. This mass movement, unexpected and unrequested, has in part caused the urban chaos that imperils those very opportunities for growth and acculturation that attracted the adventurous of former generations. Thus while the centripetal movement of the general population toward the urban areas continues unabated, it is contrasted by the opposite movement of the affluent fleeing to the suburbs. So, "safe and secure" in the suburbs, among the grass and trees and away from transportation and communication, the children and grandchildren of the adventurous have come full circle: back to the sticks and away from the big cities. Moreover numbers of them are graduating from the city-to-suburbs exodus to the city-to-wilderness pilgrimage. Colonies of young people all over the country are leaving their automated homes for the back-to-nature life.

Travel has become as much a hallmark of success in corporate America as have transfers. There is practically no prestigious job that does not put an executive on the road 20 to 30 percent of his work week. The corporate husband who is home all the time is either a nonentity or in semiretirement. Many in fact have become elite hoboes—whether solely out of corporate necessity or partly out of an unconscious desire to escape the restrictions of home life is debatable. Is staying at home really "womanish"? And in the idiom of World War II, are these trips really necessary? We do know that managerial or executive positions without travel are deemed second rate or dead-ended. The necessity of being away gives importance to a job and to an individual; it is no accident that the phrase for Mr. Success is "man on the move." An upwardly mobile young man will become highly suspicious of a company that keeps him stationary. And if he is working for a concern with widespread offices, he will see transfers as corporate recognition of his worth. Staying put means stagnation, stunting, and senescence.

For the corporate wife it is not the same. In many instances the burdens, deprivations, and penalties of moving are borne by her alone. And yet even for her there are compensations. Philosophers have long observed that the human species craves excitement. Traveling and moving, with the prospect of a new start, a new life, a new test of one's social capabilities, can be salutary to what may be called the social neurasthenia that frequently befalls stay-at-homes. Travel can be, as it has been from time immemorial, just what the doctor ordered. And as we know from history, moves from continent to continent and into undeveloped areas have been a great boon to the underclasses who could get nowhere in entrenched societies.

In the past few decades in America, Steinbeck's Okies—or a few of them—became the wealthy farmers and landowners of Arizona and California. The tale of success through moving, however, may be more myth than reality. Although purchasing land at Hollywood and Vine indeed insured future generations of wealth, nothing really produces wealth more than wealth itself. Many Okie families of the 1930s are still poor. If they did move they are now poor in California rather than Oklahoma. Yet the opportunity to strike it rich was there, in the Far West state, and not in their home territory. Those who bettered their fortunes did so because they were willing to pull up stakes.

Travel has always been the cure for the dispossessed, be they rich men's daughters or poor men's. How many young American women were shipped off to Europe after an emotional breakdown or a seige of love? The unwanted criminals of England became the barons of Australia.

The tradition of moving as a social and psychological cure is a deep one in our culture. People trapped in poverty, an immobile social status, a dying industry, a bad family name and reputation, or any of a thicket of other parochial encumbrances wrought by bias and prejudice can hope to leave much of that behind as they reach out for a fresh start. Woe to them who do not have the stamina, clear-sightedness, and courage to make a move when the cards get stacked against them. Those

40

who allow themselves to be overcome by inertia in a provincial and fixed existence may sleep their way through life.

There can be too much of a good thing, as Chapters 1 and 2 have shown; stagnation is to be abhorred, but nomadism is to be deplored. Whereas a few moves at critical times can be lifesaving, 15 or 18 in a lifetime are too many for anyone's nervous system. Perpetual wandering makes it impossible ever to unpack one's spiritual (as well as material) baggage. Yet while moving severs valuable ties and connections, it may also free one from strangling bonds.

I recall the case of a young couple driven to despair by overbearing parents who felt it their mission and obligation to run (and ruin) their lives, a story by no means singular. The young man, educated in the best schools in the East, returned to his home town, where he was expected to learn and eventually take over the family business. He married a young woman with a similar background, a union coolly accepted by both sides. They were happy in the early years of their marriage but found themselves embroiled in petty squabbles and jealousies that their respective families fomented. Each side was engaged in social climbing, literally competing with the other for community control— Capulets and Montagues in their own way.

The young couple tried to escape this struggle but were subjected to constant instigation. Each became torn between love for the spouse and family loyalty. For the young man the workday in the family business meant a barrage of insinuations about his wife and her family from his father and brothers. Trained in duty and respect, he found it increasingly difficult to ward off this onslaught, which he felt most unreasonable and unfair. Caught in a cross fire of contending interests for which he had little stomach, he became increasingly tense and anxious. He was beset by insomnia and physical complaints. Although never faltering in his devotion to his wife, he became sexually impotent. At this point he sought psychiatric help.

As his story unfolded it became apparent that he was trapped both by malignant external forces and by his own inability to free himself from them. The solution involved breaking ties better left to childhood. He was then able to muster the courage to flee the dubious security of family enticements for a new and fresh start elsewhere.

The couple made their move to a distant city where there were no family ties or influence. They were disowned by both families and struggled on their own. After a series of minor jobs, the husband was able to prove his abilities without favors or special privileges. For the first time in his life, he felt he was his own person. In all this his wife gave him the encouragement needed to dispel the self-doubts that had been

41

carefully fostered and nurtured by his overbearing parents. As he claimed his own identity, his sexual impotence disappeared, as did his other symptoms.

For some reason the achievements that come through inheritance or special advantage are never so gratifying as those conceived and won independently. And while it is true that a great many successful people who started on the shoulders of their parents went on to produce considerable and impressive accomplishments of their own, it is the self-made man who is central in the American dream. Continuing or building up a family business can be satisfying, but such successes are always somewhat diminished by the knowledge that the road was cleared by inherited power. Fathers are often perplexed and dismayed by capable sons who refuse to follow in their footsteps. Too often such fathers are trying to use their sons to perpetuate fantasies of immortality and invincibility.

Moving away solved the problem for this couple. Had they remained their lives would have been so complicated and burdened by influences and inherited expectations that their so-called advantages would have turned into irreparable handicaps.

A similar dilemma often faces the "lucky guy" who marries the daughter of the boss. This fellow is the butt of jokes, innuendos, and ridicule. These public attitudes are of course fully known to the hapless son-in-law, contributing to his existential conflict.

Such was the situation of Fred, who sought psychiatric help at the age of 40. He came in a panic with what is generally considered in psychiatry as a full-blown delusional system. He felt the people in his organization, of which he was the chief executive officer, were making horrible remarks about him. They were purportedly insinuating that he was a homosexual by making mocking gestures with their wrists. This was all so unfair, he said, because nothing could be further from the truth. A father of three healthy children, he led a full heterosexual life with his wife. He was in addition a skilled athlete and loved vigorous sports. And he was always carefully conservative in his dress and manners. How cruel then of these friends and employees to insinuate the presence of such an abnormality in him. He was desperate, trying both to convince others of his normality and to some extent to seek revenge for their slander and character assassination. He could find no reason they should turn against him in this manner. He had always gone out of his way not to offend the people at work; he had tried to be fair and generous in all his business dealings and employee relationships. This persecution by people he thought he could trust was the most disillusioning thing in his entire life. If it didn't stop he would have to run away from home and the business, to distance himself from his tormentors. Bad enough to be gossiped about, but to be accused of being a pervert was vile.

Typical of a person in such a delusional state, Fred found excuses for not confronting his accusers. For one, they never did make a direct statement but always got their message across through sly remarks and innuendos. What good would confronting them do? They would deny his accusation and then call him crazy for having such ideas. He knew of this ploy and was clever enough, he said, not to fall into that trap.

Fred did not feel that anything was wrong with his mind, but he could predict that the persistence of such persecution might indeed drive him crazy. Wasn't he beset with severe anxiety that interfered with his daily activities as well as his sleep? He had lost 20 pounds in the last two months. Only the month before he had visited a neurologist because of severe headaches that he had thought might be caused by a brain tumor. He had been reassured that there was nothing organically wrong with him. The head pain had receded.

Fred related that all the other areas of his life were problem-free. He was most successful in business, his children shunned drugs and delinquency, and his wife was loving and devoted. And up until this point he had been well-accepted by the community and was known for his generous charitable activities. A good golfer and tennis player, he was sought out as a companion by other men.

His past life was seemingly a healthy one both physically and emotionally. He had come from a poor family. His father had been a factory worker who had struggled to provide for his wife and seven children. Fred was the brightest of the children and had gone to college. He had worked his way through with part-time jobs and had graduated with honors. At college he had met his wife-to-be, Jane.

Jane was plain but intelligent and affable. Her parents, in contrast to Fred's, were quite wealthy. Her father had been head of a successful small-town business and after many years of devotion to work had wanted to retire. Having no sons, he had hoped that a son-in-law might take over.

But after marrying Jane, Fred had sought a job and been hired as a junior executive in a major national corporation. He had enjoyed his work and felt he would soon be on the way up. His job had entailed traveling; this had been upsetting to Jane. Also, living on his starting salary, Jane had had to do without many conveniences that she had been used to in her father's household. The pressure had mounted on Fred to leave his job and work with his father-in-law at a great increase in salary and with the certainty of taking over in a few years.

Fred had resisted at first, wanting to see how far he could get on his own. But the pressure had come from all sides, from his own parents as well as his wife and in-laws. This had become too much to withstand, especially now with the added expense of their children.

He had entered his father-in-law's business obligingly but with some remorse and trepidation. He had feared he would be accused of planning this right from the beginning. Smart move, marrying plain Jane! To disprove this accusation, he had worked doubly hard. His father-in-law, seeing his son-in-law's zeal and capability, had retired forthwith. Under Fred's excellent stewardship the stagnant business had prospered beyond the expectations of family and friends. From a small-town operation, it had grown to cover the entire state. Fred had indeed earned his credentials; his reputation as a capable executive was now well-established. References to marrying the boss's daughter by joking friends never had been completely extinguished, but they had seemed to die down.

Nonetheless the fact that he had come in at the top had remained a cloud over his accomplishments. Unlike Joe Lampton in the film *Room at the Top,* who seemed to have achieved his success only because he had married the boss's daughter, Fred indubitably could have made it on his own, given his drive and capability. But with his psychological makeup, derived from a background where men received credit for battles they themselves had won and where special favors were not for real men but for the effete, his successes remained questionable in his own mind. And although he was greeted by the men with respect and even affection whenever he walked through the plant or warehouse, the gnawing doubt persisted—did they still see him as the man who had married the boss's daughter?

In the course of building up his father-in-law's business, Fred had tried to assuage his feeling of discomfort by telling himself that he would stay only a few years, put the business in good shape, and then leave for a distant section of the country, where he would start from scratch. Whenever this subject had arisen, Jane had humored him—such a move would be senseless since their lives were now so comfortably built around Fred's widely acknowledged success. So he had continued building the business, winning praise, and making more money but visibly enjoying it less.

Now that he had turned 40, it had become apparent to him that he was planted. Starting anew in some other area, proving his "real worth," was impracticable. Only rarely can one start up again at this stage in life. He knew that his chance to free himself from the specter of nepotistic advantage was gone. It could now only be more of the same. All his achievements did not gratify a vital segment of Fred's character: his particular and perhaps peculiar sense of pride. Such a need to be self-made may be some vestige of an ancient culture. Nonetheless it was there to devaluate his victories.

In his symptoms Fred displayed the typical sexist attitude that there is nothing more contemptible than being a homosexual, which in turn has the connotation of being "womanish." He had made it through his father-in-law. In his sexist unconscious this meant occupying the lowly position of having received favors from a man—the normal and expected role of a woman. According to his conditioning the man who receives favors, who is given things, is not a real man. These thoughts were the source of the delusion that had overcome him, which in turn was the projection of the disdain he held for himself for having submitted to the big bribe—for having deprived himself of the challenge of making it on his own.

The causes of mental breakdowns are complex and multiple, so one can only surmise the elements that led to Fred's undoing. It is usually a combination of the past and the present resonating into a deadly result. It is virtually certain, however, that what tipped the scale in Fred's case was that he did *not* make his move.

Fred's breakdown was characterized by a severe thought disorder, which often leads to institutionalization. Luckily office psychotherapy averted this step, for Fred retained enough rational intellect and reality-testing ability to function in the world. However, his zest and enthusiasm for the business were greatly diminished. Finally he barely visited his office and entered a state of virtual retirement, spending most of his time with his family and on circumscribed community concerns in areas where he could avoid meeting his former business colleagues and employees.

Toward them he continued to feel both shame and resentment. His emotional rehabilitation was accomplished largely by a withdrawal from "the scene of the crime." Many considered him a defeated person. Others were perplexed by his paradoxical behavior—disorderly retreat in the face of victory.

Can his corporate wife, Jane, be faulted here? She liked her comforts, prestige, and family credentials and couldn't see why a new place might be any better than their town. Should she have given more attention to Fred's ego than to her own? Should she have known that his particular definition of manhood could not allow him to be the recipient of good luck from another man? Of course she would have behaved differently had she known. But we are all wise in retrospect.

As shown by the case histories in this chapter, moving can be a blessing rather than a detriment. This should come as no surprise to those who respect diversity and pluralism. The point must be emphasized, however, that one formula cannot be applied to all people. What can be a boon for some may be a bane for others; no pat generalizations can be made.

Although Vance Packard's general thesis in *A Nation of Strangers* is that the modern trend toward mobility is quite malignant, still he lists many of the arguments for moving. Some of them might be considered as rationalizations for people who need to find uses for adversity. Personal advantages range from "travel is broadening"—new faces, new friends, new opportunities—to the widened possibilities for choosing a marriage partner. Packard thinks there are advantages for the nation too: a mobile workforce is a remedy for "pockets of unemployment," more homes (and appliances and furniture) are bought, and public services are often upgraded as a byproduct.[1]

Packard quotes many famous artists and writers who appear to scoff at the idea of staying put. In *Mister Sammler's Planet* novelist Saul Bellow looks at roots as a peasant's idea—a regression for modern people. Yet for those who have studied this most thoughtful book, there is no denying that Mr. Sammler is a prime victim of uprooting, a person whose scholarly credentials were not transferable. Mr. Sammler had a planet but not a country.

Although for purposes of scholarship and fair play Packard presents the other side of the debate over mobility, he ultimately does not stray from his contention that in America today there is too much uprooting and moving for our own good. Unfortunately he does not make the distinction between those whose identities may be preserved or enhanced by moving and those whose identities may be shattered. This in turn involves the transferability of credentials as well as the participation of the affected person in the decision to change his locale. These qualitative aspects can make the move a delight or a disaster.

4

CORPORATE CHILDREN
ON THE MOVE

> *To be deeply rooted in a place that has meaning is perhaps the best gift a child can have.*
>
> CHRISTOPHER MORLEY

> *Childhood is a prison sentence of twenty-one years.*
>
> THOMAS SZASZ

CHILDREN HAVE BEEN the witnesses, beneficiaries, and victims of the uprooting and alienation that have accompanied the American success story. For the most part they have had to be passive passengers in the moves made for the survival and ambitious needs of a parent or parents. In the process children have seen their own existence battered by loss of friends, credentials, and those ballasts of community life that are needed for feelings of security and well-being.

Even the couples we saw in Chapter 2 who themselves are willing to substitute the corporation for the community are concerned about the effects of frequent transfers and moves on their children. One mother is quoted as saying, "Every time my daughter made a place for herself at school with the other kids, we'd move and she'd spend the next year trying to break in at another school. Last year, when she was a senior in high school, she had a nervous breakdown. She was sure she was an outsider."[1]

This child's experience should not be taken to mean that any move at any time is detrimental to any youngster. Although developmentally there are indeed traumas that can be injurious to a child, psychiatrists and others have exaggerated the overall effect of an individual event. We simply cannot predict with any accuracy. What one might forecast as a lasting trauma may later show no deleterious effects. Most of our clinical pronouncements on causations have been *retrospective* speculations, and the fact that they are hindsight has been largely overlooked. As a result parents today have been unduly frightened by mental hygiene and developmental phantasmagoria.

Thankfully the growing awareness of the stress on young people who must experience uprooting has led parents to seek professional advice on these matters and compare notes with other corporate families. The advice of older people, often with bitter experiences of their own, has been most helpful to their younger colleagues. A body of literature on the subject, meager at present, is beginning to appear. One such informative publication was written by Elizabeth Barnett in consultation with Dr. John E. Mack, of the Harvard Medical School.[2] The author observes that during any move it is easy for children to feel shoved aside. They are often ignored by understandably busy and preoccupied parents. There is no time to talk things over, and this results in a fearful isolation for the children.

The publication gives the sound advice to parents to discuss the move and provide full and candid explanations for it whenever possible. They should be frank about the realities of the situation; they should tell the children for example that the father did indeed lose his job rather than seek to save the family pride with a lie. Often the corporate-bred male has suffered such a loss of face through the various events of his own life that he cannot admit weakness to his family—"I can take care of everything always." The platitudes of the mother in this situation (often her husband cannot admit failure even to her) do nothing either to make the children feel that they are part of the emotional unit. When the parents' own doubts and qualms about moving (or perhaps about life in general) are made known to the children, the children are less likely to feel that they are doubters or spoilers. Indeed the truth in this instance might serve to mobilize their desire to be a part of a helpful family team. Ms. Barnett writes that "A hopeful communal spirit can emerge from helping one another through times of stress and change."

Similarly Cornell University's Professor Urie Bronfenbrenner, the noted child psychologist, warns against the isolation and alienation of children: "We isolate our children from the rest of society. There is the adult world of work and social activities, and there is the child's world of school and play with other children his or her own age. With this kind of arrangement, children have far too few opportunities to take part in the adult world."[3]

Elizabeth Barnett reminds her readers that regardless of the reason for a move, "it entails a built-in and undesirable sense of loss."[4] Each member of the family will feel it in his own way, and periods of depression are unavoidable. Depression may manifest itself in irritability, acting out of sorts, or a quarrelsome disposition. These traits may appear instead of the dark mood and tears generally associated with depression. This is especially important to know since many people feel distressingly inadequate or incompetent when these symptoms do appear. Instead one should realize that the manifestations are normal for the circumstance.

The essay goes on to describe the reaction of children in various age groups. The author states that one of the greatest fears of the 18-month-old toddler is that he will be abandoned. But it appears from the literature that the most stressful periods for moves are the ages 3 to 5 and 14 to 16. Naturally there are exceptions; some parents report that their children moved easily at these ages, and some cite other periods as difficult. There is also a sex difference—at certain points male children might be able to move more readily than females, for reasons that will be given later. Of course matters of preparation, cooperation, consent, and distance can either mitigate or augment stresses. But from the reports that have come to me through the years, these two age groups appear to have the greatest problems. The 3- to 5-year-olds have internal troubles; the 14- to 16-year-olds suffer largely from social frustrations.

Although at the earlier ages anxiety might be aroused by the loss of the security derived from familiar people and surroundings, little children's fears and consequent sufferings when moving are caused largely by misinformation and by misinterpretations arising from the fantasy world young children occupy. Often they interpret a move as punitive, as an act of hostility on the part of the powerful, world-shaking parents. Also the move is often incorporated into the child's primitive theories of existence, with at times frightening effects.

One such child shortly before an anticipated move reverted to bed-wetting and night terrors that necessitated psychiatric consultation. His parents had done all the right things in preparing him for the move. But as is so often the case, preparation, good intentions, and love were not enough to deal with the strength of the inner forces of the child's imagination. What was finally uncovered proved to be of great help in treating him.

There had been a loss in the family—a favorite grandparent had died. In explaining this tragedy to the child, the mother characteristically stated that Grandmother had "gone to heaven." This euphemism seemed to satisfy the youngster since it harmonized with his Sunday school information. But it unfortunately became connected gratuitously with another incident. A neighbor was visiting the household, and naturally the imminent move was the topic of the conversation, which the youngster was privy to. "Oh, how I envy you," the neighbor exclaimed. "I was there; I found it *heavenly*." That is all the child needed to feel that they were all going to be with Grandmother—all die! After dispelling his fears on this score, the parents made the move. Although the nocturnal disturbances persisted for a while, they disappeared without any lasting ill effects.

It is dangerous to use euphemisms and flowery language around children; theirs is largely a concrete, literal world. Obviously the death in the family was a stressful factor all on its own for a child at that age. Juxtaposed to a family move, it became emotionally overwhelming.

The grade school child is likely to take a negative attitude about everything in the new area—school, teacher, playground, and so on. This reflects his insecurity probably more than the actual state of things. It is recommended that when possible parents write ahead to the school principal to learn of the curriculum, supplies required, and even manner of dress. This forearming may make it easier for the child to catch on more easily.

There are instances where a change of locus might be marvelously beneficial to children. This might be so for a child who is captive to the torments of peers and even teachers.

To one boy in anguish moving brought at least temporary relief. For this child of an executive in an electronics firm, the prospect of going to another place and having a new beginning was his sole chance for survival.

Jim was an only child, born late in life to adoring parents. But unfortunately he was beset with physical problems. From the age of 6 to 14, he was extremely obese. In addition his eyesight was impaired, requiring him to wear thick glasses. As if these were not enough, he was flat-footed; as he said, he could neither run nor walk. Because he was big and looked burly, his schoolmates and teachers expected some athletic capability; he had none. Each time he went to gym class, he was derided by the others. Even the more charitable teachers had to hide their disgust. Only rarely would a fellow student or teacher express some sympathy for his plight. Yet despite continual torment he persisted in gym without resorting to a doctor's excuse.

His parents seemed helpless to improve the situation, but sensing their son's awful predicament, they deliberately transferred to a new district of the corporation whenever the opportunity arose. Here was an instance where an executive sought to be moved by his company for the sake of his family. Ironically he was given no great promotions, because the corporation viewed his desire to move with suspicion. Apparently moving for the benefit of the firm shows loyalty, elasticity, and adaptability, whereas initiating a change for private, family reasons places one under suspicion if not in jeopardy.

For Jim each move brought temporary relief from persecution and hope for a fresh start. As soon as his awkwardness was discovered, however, he was subjected to ridicule. Although most boys are not star athletes, each is expected to at least perform in gym. The chubby, near-sighted, clumsy boy is subjected to the same kind of torment as is the girl who simply is not pretty or—ironically—who looks "unfeminine" and is a crack athlete.

Jim tried to improve himself in any way—with exercises and instructions—but to little avail. Finally at 14 he put himself on a crash diet and succeeded in losing 75 pounds. Doing this, however, he developed a gastrointestinal disorder for which he had to be hospitalized. After he recovered he was able to maintain his new weight. He became more physically attractive, but he was left with psychic scars from the lacerating experiences of his earlier childhood.

The issue of transfer of credentials may be crucial for adolescents who must move with their family. This, a form of personal hijacking, makes them helpless captives of the will of others. Forced to the road by the parents, who themselves were forced, the young person may take refuge in uncharacteristic behavior.

The complicating factors of mating and dating come to the fore in the teen years as do heightened skills and abilities, both academic and extracurricular. These of course contribute to identity formation and ego gratification. Therefore loss of some or all of these can and does cause trouble of major proportions.

If adults suffer from losing friends and confidants, with adolescents the situation is sometimes calamitous. Imagine having to be separated from the most popular boy in the school just as he is beginning to pay attention to you. Many a teenage girl balks at the prospect—she just won't move. Can we blame her? The mating game is too precarious for her to be reassured that Mr. Dreamboat will reappear at the next high school. Or imagine the boy who is about to quarterback the football team of his school. Try to persuade him that this will happen in Podunk! Or take a talented daughter away from a ballet school, of which there are likely to be none in Florence, Arizona. Family loyalty and solidarity are likely to go down the drain in these instances, especially when the youth is spirited and motivated.

Studies seem to highlight peer acceptance and confirmation as necessities for proper emotional and intellectual growth. Although one would hope that growing up healthy would depend on more than popularity, this dimension is very real indeed for young people—not that it is by any means absent from their parents' lives.

Most of us in growing up are ordinary and unbeautiful. Therefore we usually cannot risk losing the peer supports that we do have. When these supports are taken away, there is loneliness and even despair.

In many instances an adolescent has already been subjected to many moves. When parents attempt or are forced into another transfer, they may find that the kids elect to remain with friends or relatives, run away, or do any one of the thousand other parent-injuring activities open to them. And paradoxically defiance may be far healthier than the passive abandonment of the social supports that he or she has gained and often desperately needs to sustain the ego. More often than not both conventional and psychiatric wisdom calls the rebellious or defiant youth "disturbed" or "deviant." On the contrary this stubbornness on the part of young people may indicate that they in truth have minds of their own. For an autonomous person personal values must at times preempt family loyalty and even love. There are probably more untoward reactions among the cooperative than among the defiant.

What can be done if a child is distressed by moving? Parents should of course try every device to help her or him adjust to the new environment and retain important ties with the old, by visits to friends for example. But perhaps the idea of letting the child finish the scholastic year surrounded by old friends and sustained by school community status is a good one. Living with friends or neighbors and rejoining the family later may turn out to be not only a reasonable solution to the transfer-of-credentials problem but a valuable lesson in independence and autonomy. Holding on to the adolescent, forcing the child to remain close to the family in its moves, may exact an attrition of its own even though there is an outward appearance of togetherness.

There is the case for instance of a 15-year-old daughter who had made five moves with her family and would not make the sixth in her sophomore year in high school. The parents arranged to board her in the neighborhood where she lived. She continued at the same school, where she did well academically and was very popular. After graduation she went on to college. At the time her parents were dismayed and chided her for her disloyalty. But it was her dutiful, docile mother who later became depressed and suicidal.

Not to go is a most difficult decision to make—young adolescents still need family security and support. They do not want to inflict harm. They are not engaged in neurotic life-and-death struggles with parents.

Abandoning the family takes a special strength. But parents do not always know best.

Parents are usually advised that no moves should be made during a school semester since the academic disruption can result in the loss of a full school year, a harsh risk for a marginal student. In addition a transfer in the senior year has proved to be a particular hardship for many young people. At such times strong friendships and love relationships may have been formed. Senior-year status and leadership positions are often important factors. Moving may constitute a literal tearing away, with Romeo and Juliet results.

The following recounts the diverse reactions of two young people, twins, aged 17. Both bright and precocious, they moved with their parents just before their senior year. The boy was a star athlete, a football player, who had made the all-county team the previous year. The coach at the new school sought him out as soon as his arrival became known; his ability raised the hopes of the football team for the regional championship. For this young man, who had no difficulty transferring his now considerable credentials, the move led to happiness and enhancement.

His twin sister was not so fortunate. A good student but without exceptional abilities or attributes, she had no brass band to meet her. She left her high school sorority, of which she had been president. She left a boyfriend, whose interest could not be sustained over a distance of 2,000 miles. At the new school it was too late to develop meaningful relationships or gain a position in extracurricular organizations. As if this was not enough, her academic standing, in which she took pride, fell because of different standards in the two states. She was no longer an honor student and was thus disqualified from some of the prizes for excellence that she had secretly hoped to win.

After the move a noticeable change took place in her. Never an extrovert, she now became increasingly withdrawn, remaining in her room most of the time and staying away from school, church, and other activities she had usually pursued. Her parents were helpless to influence her new behavior. Responding to the contemporary fears, they accused her of taking drugs, but this was not so. She was much too angry for that. Finally she agreed to see a psychotherapist, to whom she was eventually able to relate.

In the course of therapy, she was able to express her deep bitterness about what had been done to her. Furthermore she was able to resolve that never again would she allow obedience and docility to prevail over self-preserving preferences. She later married and also pursued a career. She made certain that after marriage she would not be subjected to major displacements or inordinate sacrifices. Her adolescent experience and the insight she gained as a result of therapy served to arm her for the struggles that were to come.

Her twin brother continued to experience a smooth and uneventful passage through adolescence and adult life. He became an attorney and never did resist the flow of his considerable advantages, some earned, some unwon. Although the young man exceeded every American standard for success and his sister by contrast provoked worry and uncertainty, the very smoothness of his life led to a shallowness and insensitivity that made him a less interesting and less compassionate person.

Nonetheless, in terms of the immediate effect of the move, the boy's popularity was luckily transferable. He might have had grave difficulties if for instance he had been an average football player and had not made the team. The fact that he was a star made the move a successful one. This was very good luck, for most adolescents (and adults) are not stars and become silent social and psychological casualties. Furthermore, when a star can make it, this does not mean that those who don't are weak or inept, as is often inferred even by loving parents.

In retrospect the plight of the young woman reveals the fragility of the process of adolescence, a period in life when doubt and uncertainty about self are already so extreme that added pressures may exhaust the adaptive energies of the organism.

To those who have felt unduly manipulated, transported against their will, or uprooted to their disadvantage, the recourse frequently is withdrawal and self-exile from the family and community. It is a form of passive resistance as old as history itself. In the *Iliad* we read of Achilles petulantly retreating to his tent as an expression of grievance against the Greek high command. Children are of course told, "Go to your room," as an indication of parents' disappointment. It is a sophisticated punishment, a temporary exile until the child can "think things over." It gives the child an opportunity for self-reflection, which the parents hope will produce a modified attitude or behavior that will be more consonant with their wishes. A child's self-exile on the other hand causes great consternation, as it did in the case of the girl twin. Exile by authority figures is considered normal and appropriate; to do it to oneself on the contrary is seen as an indication of uncooperativeness and even sickness.

The room then is an escape from oppressive conditions, a last resort if you will to preserve integrity and sanity. A last resort, that is, bar one—the withdrawal from life itself. When worldly opportunities for enhancement and assertion are diminished or frustrated beyond a certain point, living often becomes unbearable. This is why the suicide risk among adolescents is so great. It is a reason that they take such inordinate chances with their lives through alcohol, drugs, and fast cars. Many of the highway accidents may indeed be hidden suicides. Japan and the Scandinavian countries have experienced this tragedy for several decades. It may be spreading to America.

At the fourth congress of the Union of European Pedopsychiatrists, Dr. Maija-Liisa Koski of the University Children's Hospital of Turku, Finland, reported a study dealing with the psychological factors observed in 15 suicidal children 10 to 15 years of age. She pointed out that they and later adolescents often live under what may be considered two contradictory standards simultaneously, one created by parents and the other created by friends. Dr. Koski is quoted as saying, "If the adolescent experiences frustrations and desertions in both of these 'Worlds,' death might come to his mind as the only possible solution under the pressure of loneliness and nonlove."[5]

Obviously withdrawal from either world is an option that most young people do not take. Another escape route is open to them.

Running away from home—whether as a valid attempt to escape from a burning building, a temporary expedient or power play, or an expression of a healthy maturing process and a desire to seek autonomy in the world—has been part of the human scene from time immemorial. Today masses of young people have taken to the road to escape what they feel are social oppressions as well as to seek different life styles more consonant with changing times and mores. Most, like prodigal sons and daughters, will return to the fold in one way or another, but some will not be heard from again—devoured by unjust laws and practices that their parents never bothered to change.

A child's departure from home into a life on his or her own is rarely easy for parents to accept. Whatever the reason for the leavetaking, they see it as an alienation, a crystallizing of the gap in communication they may have felt between themselves and the child for years. T. S. Eliot writes of this isolation:

> Two people who know they do not understand each other,
> Breeding children whom they do not understand
> And who will never understand them.[6]

These lines perceive the vast gaps that exist between even those who live together in the closest proximity. At best we all muddle through; only exceptionally does the human experiment really succeed. It is true that most of us spend our lives cohabitating with people we really never get to know, having and raising children who become strangers to us. It is little wonder then that so few people feel successful as parents.

55

They end up dissatisfied with either the way they have behaved or the way their children have turned out. It is the rule to hear parents say, "Where did I go wrong?" or "My children are disappointments to me." Of course one must keep in mind that either complaint may simply reflect the parents' unhappiness that the child had not turned out the way they want. The son who becomes a painter or a poet instead of going into his father's business may eclipse his father by far in worldly contributions, but he rarely measures up in his father's eyes.

Today, with the emergence of the counterculture, there are thousands of parents who have written off sons and daughters because the young people have chosen life styles so alien as to make contacts—not to speak of communication—distasteful or even totally untenable. This alienation between the generations has spared no social or economic class. Sons and daughters of our top executives inhabit caves and communes or wander the earth. Whatever happened to the gray flannel suit of the 1940s? Executives' children wear patched blue jeans and torn sneakers. The search is no longer for where the grass is greener but where it is stronger. Children whose grandparents used to grow their own food, weave their own cloth, and doctor themselves are indeed doing that again. Their parents, who had so proudly sent them to Harvard and Smith, watch with amazement as they build latrines and bake bread.

Only those corporate parents with strong egos and creative imaginations have been able to accept this state of things as a constructive evolution. Only a few have been able to see their children in terms of Consciousness III, the term supplied by Charles Reich to label the new philosophy of living.

In traveling and wandering as they do, the children may in fact be imitating their parents and paradoxically be dutiful and loyal kids after all. Certainly many of the counterculture youths moved quite a bit with their corporate parents and are unafraid of the road and new places. Why then should the parents become so upset when they themselves established the tradition? Haven't we been told that imitation is the sincerest form of flattery? Yes, but the parents observe, "We did it responsibly and with a goal." Yet the precedent for movement was established, and the freedom to wander was fully experienced in childhood. However, there are reservations about the efficacy of that sense of responsibility and that goal.

There is no doubt that many of these "errant" children will return to the fold and even to the executive suite. Many on the other hand will be permanently lost to the parental way of life. And who is to deny that from these something better or more viable may emerge?

56

Corporate children have been witnesses to the discord and suffering of parents who have often been destroyed by the very success that was to save them. Marriage and conventional family living have little appeal for many young people today, having seen the disasters in their own well-fitted but ill-fated homes.

Their desire to carry on in the style of their parents has been considerably dampened. Young men and women are drifting away from the lives of achievement and power; success is not the golden calf that it was to their parents. For whether young people are correct in their protest, they have been hurt by what they themselves have experienced. It is not likely that personal advancement and monetary gain will be the sole determinants of how they will live.

Young people, as part of their identification with life-giving and life-promoting forces, want to correct inequities and to undo oppressive forces. In this they would like to have their own parents as models. Sadly it has often been most difficult to find models among parents. Marvelous in matters of production and sales, corporate parents as a group have not been in the forefront with regard to the pressing moral issues of the day. They were not among the first to speak out against poverty, racism, sexism, and our great tragedy in Vietnam. Their role in the peace movement was less than it might have been.

Their attention to environmental problems has left something to be desired. Although they themselves are always impeccably dressed and their lawns clear of crabgrass, their industrial plants pollute the air, the land, and our waterways. Ironically it is not the hippies who have dirtied our nation. Who is to say that being spaced out is a lesser position morally than taking up all the space? Ecologically the achievers and producers are now viewed as polluters. Josephine W. Johnson, Pulitzer Prize novelist, writes: "It is the well-dressed, law-abiding, patriotic and upright citizens who are taking our country away from us. In the name of saving us, protecting us, statesmen and generals, scientists and engineers, businessmen and Congressmen, are making us a people without a country, dead souls and exiles. And we are paying to do it."[7]

Even if the pollution and the destruction were not done with malice, such lack of interest, unconcern, and bad judgment have the effect of lessening the credibility of parents in the eyes of their children. They figure they can hardly do so badly and will pose far less threat to human values and the environment if they simply sit around playing the guitar. Accused by their annoyed elders of irresponsibility and laziness young people—with much justification—feel that the real practitioners of the copout are the "busy."

This apparent turning away from parental values of success and achievement is massive in America today. The number of eager young team players who will be sent anywhere anytime for the corporate good is diminishing among the young, despite job scarcity and unemployment at present. Problems of boredom and listlessness in both the blue- and the white-collar groups are being reported with alarm. Similarly our Department of Commerce warns of diminishing productivity rates that may place the United States at a disadvantage in world markets. Increased productivity and growth, the very pride of American life, are being challenged by the young, who are clearly disappointed with the end results of growth and success.

Perhaps "success" and what one has to do for it have produced a pollution within family life and interpersonal relations that is as damaging socially and psychologically as what the smokestacks and effluent drains have wrought in the environment.

PART II

Contexts and Causes

5

BULLS IN THE CHINA SHOP

In traditional corporate law, property is defined as things (res), but the major lesson which corporations have learned in the last 30 years is that a corporation, while producing things, is made up of people, and that one cannot treat people—at least managerial and white collar personnel—as things.

DANIEL BELL

IN HIS EXCELLENT BOOK *Anxiety and the Executive,* Alan N. Schoonmaker comments that in 1969 even the major corporations of America were relatively indifferent to the impact of their personnel practices—such as transferring employees—on wives and families. Dr. Schoonmaker writes:

> The company attitude is that a wife must move without complaint to wherever the corporation wants to send her husband, be cheerful and gracious when he brings home unexpected guests (even if she dislikes them), accept his long hours and company travel with a smile, run her house like a branch office, express the proper political and economic attitudes, drop her old friends as he moves up, and change her personality and habits, if necessary, to fit in with his job and associates. In other words, she is allowed to have no needs or personality of her own, because her husband's career is more important than she is.[1]

There are strong indictments against the hand that feeds. And today with Naderism and other vocal consumer movements, it is quite fashionable to attack our Goliaths. Nor do all the attacks come from the little guy's corner. David Rockefeller, chairman of the board of the Chase Manhattan Bank, writes that businessmen and industrialists have been slow to interest themselves in the social problems of the day. He asks, "Will business leaders seize the initiative to make necessary changes

61

and take on new responsibilities voluntarily, or will they wait until these are thrust upon them by law?"

And in looking to the future, Mr. Rockefeller, no Jerry Rubin, makes the prediction: "Because of the growing pressure for greater corporate accountability I can foresee the day when corporations may be required to publish a 'social audit' certified by independent accountants."[2]

Before we start throwing stones, let us recognize that big business, as much as other institutions of our country, has suffered from the cultural lag that is now becoming so apparent in many areas. In the struggle for survival and growth, human values are often forgotten, just as ecological considerations were largely overlooked in the past decades, a neglect for which we are now paying an awesome price. Corporations have erred without malice—they do not deliberately plan hardships for their employees. And our corporations are not social agencies engaged in either the prevention or the cure of the emotional problems of workers and their families. The driving force of modern industry is in the realm of economics, not sociology or psychology. The way companies help is through the paycheck or extramonetary benefits. By and large this is how it should be. More extensive help could smack of paternalism; a firm could be meddling in the private affairs of its employees.

Yet short of converting every executive chair into a psychoanalyst's couch, companies could do more without the danger of going soft or of indulging their help. The entire country today is weary of "growth" and "progress." People want more attention paid to human values and the quality of living. Our top-notch corporation executives are acutely cost-conscious about plant maintenance, personnel, and product, as they should be. Yet heightened attention to the human cost in industrial management is an idea whose time has come. And it might just be good (and profitable) business practice if for instance General Electric added one word before its well-known slogan so that it proclaimed: "Human progress is our most important product."

For many employees, as Chapter 2 discussed, the corporation often must be the substitute for all those social and community supports that have to be left behind or that in another day emanated from the richness of traditional rootedness. Therefore the company must supply more than salaries to employees and goods and services to customers. It literally must be a satisfying and enjoyable institution for its own. Although a university's primary job is to educate, it must also provide a campus where faculty and students may live in relative harmony, happiness, and security. Corporations need not be halfway houses or substitute moms and pops for homesick waifs, but they do have the moral obligation to provide opportunities for gratifying experiences of living, which in turn

62

help employees and spouses maintain their sense of integrated person-hood. Too big an order? Paternalism? Do-goodism? No, enlightened self-interest. And yes, patriotism. Corporate America is America for a large share of its own citizenry. Where else can people go for liveli-hood and involvement?

There are strong indications that corporate America isn't meeting its responsibilities to itself and its own. Pollster George Gallup, Jr., told an American Management Associations seminar on productivity in 1972 that job dissatisfaction among young workers poses a growing threat to the country's productivity.[3] His surveys revealed that over all 19 per-cent of American workers of all ages were currently unhappy in their jobs. However, in the 18- to 29-year-old age group, 33 percent consid-ered their jobs unsatisfactory. These young workers admitted to loafing on the job: 70 percent felt that they weren't producing to full capacity. And 52 percent of all age groups believed they could be producing more. Young people particularly were dissatisfied with "urban industrial areas" with five-day workweeks.

Unhappiness and discontent generally don't worry us (we scoff at such subjective laments), but sagging productivity does. In the instance of the Gallup findings, the economic aspects of the problem got the newspaper headline: "Unhappy Young Workers Called Threat to Out-put." So did it in this front-page news item—"Divorce Rise Among Managers Curbs the Effectiveness of Some Executives":

> Absenteeism [and] inefficiency increase in managerial ranks as more are faced with divorce, gripe many employers. "The problem is getting worse all the time," complains one. At one big Midwest electronics firm, the performance of a middle manager ebbs as his wife mulls divorce. "He's not with it," says an official; "he can't meet deadlines." A big enginemaker demotes a financial officer plagued by similar woes.
>
> Personnel men blame the rise on the "increasing pressures" of business, such as more frequent executive transfers. "Women feel, to hell with it," says one; they "can't put up with it." Most firms stay out of the executives' private lives. But Litton Industries offers voluntary counseling to employees with marital troubles. Its goal: to assist them to regain their "normal performance level."
>
> Yet divorce doesn't always lower managerial output; the perfor-mance of one Midwest executive showed "drastic improvement" after his wife divorced him.[4]

Output problems catch the corporate eye first. These must be reme-died, and if workers become happier in the course of the correction, all to the good. Would there be any interest in the unhappiness of young workers or the rising divorce rate among managers if there were no threat to output? Gallup might make a study of this among top executives. The economic goals, those of profit and production, are there indisputably; about the social objectives, those of helping employees infuse meaning and gratification into their lives, there is considerable doubt. It will be a pleasant lesson and reward of the future if the economic and social modes, far from being antagonistic, march together.

The "social audit" that David Rockefeller foresees might begin with a hard look at the family-dividing aspects of employees' jobs. In the past, as Schoonmaker indicates, personnel have been moved like pawns without request or consultation and with little or no regard for the personal family problems that were created. Then there is the matter of business trips, not only in themselves but in the economic disparity that the ubiquitous expense account introduces into a couple's life. Especially if he is a young man, it allows the husband to enjoy a higher standard of living away from than at home. Over a period of time, despite protests to the contrary, the road with all its attendant loneliness and other purported hardships may eclipse the attractions of home because it affords a life high on the hog that is unavailable on the family budget. Wives sadly indulge in wishful thinking when they relate how miserable their husband is when traveling, how he misses home cooking, how lumpy and cold single hotel beds must be. These frequently are self-consoling cover stories to hide an all too real inequity. For the young, lower-income corporate male, the Internal Revenue Service with its business-deductible allowances creates still another advantage that can turn his head.

Attention from secretaries and airline stewardesses, the luxuries of first-class hotels, the excitement engendered by Playboy entertainment, rental limousines, expense account filet mignon, and other privileges of business trips leave their marks. It is not too long before the husband feels that he really deserves advantages unavailable to his mate. There is a definite corrupting influence here at work: "I must be great if I am being treated so well." A regrettable consequence of this self-deception is that wife Jane becomes identified with her inferior hamburgers and loses out in the competition between home and roam. Husband then perfunctorily pays lip service to the virtues of home (rhetoric for home consumption) but often can't wait to hit the road again, where he lives sumptuously. If there are some tinges of guilt about this inequity, he has the convenient rejoinder that he is forced into it as part of his job. If our welfare system places a monetary advantage on fathers' abandoning their wives and children, the expense account, with the Internal Revenue Service regulations on it, is making its contribution to middle-class family wrecking.

The comparison is not unintentional: money—or the way it is distributed in our big-business economy—is perhaps the single largest cause of family breakups in our nation. In the lower socioeconomic groups, financial pressures cause fathers to abandon their families because they cannot take the humiliation of being unable to provide for their children as a man purportedly should. Undoubtedly factors other than financial play large roles in these instances of desertion, but one of these is attributable to American business: its neglect until recent years to hire and advance people without regard to race, religion, and other elements of background. The poor in this country are largely minority-group members.

Among middle- and upper-class parents, overt abandonment is rare. Yet the well-to-do corporate executive may be as errant as his poorer brother. His business trips, always necessities, keep him from parenthood to almost the same point as does the poverty of the hapless ghetto deserter. Unimpeachable in his attention to the material well-being of his wife and children, he deserts them emotionally. How ironic it is that the ghetto father abandons his family because he is a financial failure and the corporate executive because of his success!

As previous chapters have pointed out, neither business trips nor transfers seem avoidable in these days of far-flung enterprises. But surely the personal desires and needs of employees could be given greater consideration than at present. Reluctance to travel or to move has always been interpreted as lack of loyalty or poor motivation. A reluctant employee would be either fired or marked for oblivion as far as further responsibilities or opportunities were concerned. Only exceptionally, with an indispensable person such as a genius inventor, would dissent be tolerated. We can do better. There can be consultations with the employee so that he can present his case when he feels a move will be inordinately burdensome to him or members of his family. And a move might be delayed or canceled without stigmatization of the employee. With some faith in the goodwill and honest intentions of employees—and these virtues are commoner than we credit—corporations may benefit greatly by enhanced loyalty and respect of workers. A man can hardly have anything but ambivalent feelings toward a company that has torn his family apart.

Business trips and transfers may wreak the greatest hardships on the wife and children, but even within the job context, they can put considerable stress on the executive himself. In a letter to the editor responding to my article "Dear Mr. Success . . . ," Miles Duley emphasized the distress that a move can cause a man:

Dr. Seidenberg has taken one isolated situation and projected it as a normal problem for progressing executives. The burden is as heavy to bear for the husband as it is for the wife. Any executive who is promoted and relocates does so with a degree of mixed emotion for himself and his family. Past achievements do not guarantee future success even in his present company. He must prove himself every time he is promoted. Therefore, the pressures are equally distributed to both husband and wife. Those who pursue status and recognition above self-fulfillment create their own hell. Any wife whose husband steps upon the corporate ladder confronts relocation and adjustment. When first married she will inwardly rebel when her husband takes her away from her family and her contact with them is reduced because of distance, even if that distance is only 100 miles. I have seen men become bitter and rejected because of wives who refuse to relocate and in essence seal off the future dreams and ambitions of their husbands. The relocation of a family should be approached by husband and wife with a positive outlook and not one of negative retrenchment. Ties will be severed and friends will be removed, but not forgotten. New experiences and friends await those who relocate. The horizons can hold new adventures if the mind is not fenced in by the past. Dr. Seidenberg is correct in stating that the husband has a responsibility to his wife in consulting her in the uprooting of a family; but if maturity and objectivity is lacking on either part, then successful relocation may be conceived but will never bear fruit.[5]

Miles Duley tells us that the male in corporate America has no bed of roses placed before him. He reminds us of the struggles, uncertainties, and disappointments that face him not only with every move but in everyday life. There is no disputing this point. Dr. Schoonmaker tells us of the deleterious effects of uprooting on the American executive:

> This constant moving has an even more serious effect: it prevents some executives from developing close friendships or real roots in any community. Because they know they will be moving again someday, they keep themselves and their families mobile. They don't become really involved in any community or get too close to anyone in it. . . . Their friends are usually people like themselves—families on the move—and everyone follows the same rules in these friendships. The principle may be stated as: "Be friendly, but not too friendly, because someday you will have to say good-bye." . . . Their superficial relationships, shallow roots, and noninvolvement keep them mobile and advance their careers but also create loneliness and anxiety.[6]

Chapter 2, in discussing the human need for credentials and community, gave several examples of how this "loneliness and anxiety" have affected men's thinking and feelings. But William Christensen and Lawrence Hinkle have found that the stress on corporate executives is

66

considerable in terms of physical afflictions as well as social and psychological malaise.[7] Theirs is a fascinating study, one of the few that show social cause and physical effect clearly.

Christensen and Hinkle found marked differences in the prevalence of disease between a group of managers who had completed college and those doing the same job for the same pay in the same company but who had not finished college before coming into the industry. There were other marked social differences between the two groups. Those who had completed college were generally fourth-generation Americans, sons of managers, proprietors, and white-collar workers, and had grown up in relative affluence with the social and educational advantages that go with it. Those who had not completed college had originally been hired as skilled workers and had risen to managerial or executive levels. These were the sons or grandsons of immigrants who themselves had had little education and had been unskilled workers. The neighborhoods in which they were raised were often substandard and offered inferior educational opportunities. Later in life, it was shown, these sons of immigrants had a significantly greater number of physical illnesses than did the members of the advantaged group. Apparently lack of preparation and the struggle upward with its attendant anxieties takes its toll by wearing down organs and arteries. One can surmise that the rags-to-riches self-made man has to run plenty scared, with little margin for error.

This certainly confirms Miles Duley's observation that the male striving to make something of himself has a bumpy road indeed. And in the struggle to keep his own body and soul together, he may have no energy left for concern about a wife's identity problems or the nuances of psychological strain on the children.

As if to do penance for sundering executives from their wives and children, some large corporations are moving their principal offices to the suburbs. The exodus to the pastoral areas has been a mixed blessing—it has created what might be labeled "corporate loneliness." Deirdre Carmody reported on the decisions made by two giant firms: Joseph E. Seagram and Sons, which chose to remain in New York City after contemplating a move; and PepsiCo, which moved out of its Manhattan offices into a $20 million complex in Purchase, New York.[8]

Seagram decided to stay in the city and lease more space following a survey of 17 executives the majority of whom commuted daily from their homes in the suburbs. While the company's study found that relocating in the suburbs would not result in any financial saving, one of the chief reasons for remaining was the mental isolation that such a move would engender. The report stated: "If employees dealt almost exclusively with others from the company, there would be a tendency to reinforce existing thought patterns; there would be a danger of mental lethargy. In the long run, this would have a deleterious effect on productivity." With this one can heartily agree. Would that a similar solicitude be felt toward suburban wives who experience this lethargy every day of their lives!

At Purchase the 1,200 executives and secretaries responded anonymously with general enthusiasm over corporate life in the suburbs. According to Victor Bonomo, a PepsiCo vice president, the move has been a success. It is claimed that recruiting personnel has been made easier, and productivity has increased. But perceptive Mr. Bonomo admits that a price has been paid for this isolation from city life: "You tend to talk to yourselves. . . . You've got to work at it to avoid inbreeding, to avoid looking out of the window at how good life is, to avoid looking out at the crabapples in bloom."

On the positive side, another PepsiCo official noted that commuting time has diminished, allowing him to eat dinner with his family for the first time in years. He comments that there is less strain and hopefully less wear and tear on the body and nervous system as a consequence of the proximity of his home to the office. Certainly he has a point, and the corporation's move may be a step toward sustaining family unity. However, the consequences of the mental isolation and "inbreeding" may greatly outweigh such benefits. We will have to wait and see whether such moves produce a new syndrome of corporate loneliness parallel to the personal deprivation suffered by so many suburban-based wives.

There is as well a sensitive and gnawing moral question connected with moving to the suburbs. The Right Rev. Paul Moore, Jr., on being enthroned as the thirteenth Episcopal bishop of New York, lamented: "Our sin is not as colorful as Sodom's but deeper. It is the sin of Cain, the murder of our brothers. New York murders her children in the tenements, on the streets, in the schools, while those who can escape understandably seek an illusory Eden in the suburbs."[9] How much responsibility corporations or individual executives must take for contributing to the quality of life in cities has only recently come into the public debate. If the environment protection movement is any indication, however, big business is likely to find itself held increasingly accountable for the welfare not only of its immediate employees and their families but also of those who ultimately pay it its income—the public at large.

Again, consideration of human and social needs is entirely possible without softening or weakening of corporate structure. In their often indifferent and callous attitude toward these matters, corporations may be conforming with what might be called corporate *machismo*—an unnecessarily he-man approach to problems where compassion and understanding would actually accomplish much more.

In an effort to learn more about current practices, I sent letters of inquiry to 50 of America's leading corporations, asking them what they do to alleviate the burdens specifically of moving for their employees. From their replies and personal interviews, I am somewhat more optimistic today than Dr. Schoonmaker was in 1969. Most companies are beginning to recognize the problem and in limited ways are trying to help. They are becoming increasingly openhanded in lessening the financial hardships of moving.

Another survey in 1972 showed that the average coverage of transfer expenses had risen 44 percent, from $2,459 to $3,539, since a year earlier. A growing number of corporations assist in house sales. One employer in three will take title to an old house; another third of the companies surveyed will cover any loss from the sale. Also allowances are now more liberal for meals, motels, maid service, house hunting, and appliance service.[10]

Several of the firms to which I wrote issue booklets with helpful hints and suggestions as well as outlines of what the family can expect in the way of reimbursement. One corporation employs a psychiatrist as a consultant in these matters. In others personnel directors try to do what they can in the way of counseling. At least one major corporation, IBM, has begun inviting the employee and spouse to visit the proposed new community, which the couple may decline to move to without retribution. The company does not now cavalierly order people to a new location. Although no panacea, such a policy is an enlightened one that deserves broad adoption by others. Can one convincingly say that such participation in decision making will topple IBM?

In their zeal, many firms have advocated hiring company psychologists or psychiatrists to offer therapy or counseling to employees, spouses, and children on any problems, including those related to corporate practices. This would be a mistake. Although such professional help might be sought out by management in helping them regarding personnel policy and other corporate matters, therapy provided by staff professionals would entail a conflict of interest for both therapist and patient that would vitiate any possible benefits. The patient could never really feel that the company's practitioner would remain neutral or objective, and the practitioner would be placed in an untenable moral and ethical position. Feeling a need for treatment, an employee or spouse should seek out private help in the community with a professional person who has no connection with either the family itself or the corporation. The resulting privacy enhances the trust and confidence that are the sine qua non of an effective therapeutic relationship.

The issue of psychological privacy in industry is one that has been looming over the horizon for several decades. In 1951 William H. Whyte, Jr., found that during the hiring procedure, one-half of the corporations made wife screening a regular practice, and at least 20 percent of the acceptable trainees were turned down because of the bad impression made by their wives.[11] In addition to interviewing the spouses, Whyte found, many hiring executives made home calls. Some brought their own wives along to make judgments as only "one woman can about another." One college president boasted that before hiring a new faculty or administrative staff member, he insisted on having breakfast with the candidate's family. It was his judgment that if the wife "didn't fix her husband a good breakfast," the man "wasn't a good risk." Personnel departments often sent wives to corporation psychologists for the purpose of eliminating job applicants whose spouses were prone to nagging, resistant to the husband's traveling, or likely to succumb to alcohol or sexual dalliances.

After a man was hired, the problem of how far the wife should be integrated into the corporation arose. Should she not be a secret salesman or loyal ambassador whenever the occasion arose? Many companies periodically distributed booklets to wives informing them of the altruistic efforts and community contributions of the company that might be mentioned at bridge and cocktail parties. A wife could be considered in a more active role too. She might join with her husband in the edification and entertaining of customers in order to get a difficult order or close a deal. She might be the one to tip the scale positively on that million-dollar insurance policy. Other companies frowned on any active participation of wives other than through normal entertaining. In these cases the wife did her duty by being as unobtrusive as possible.

Recognizing the unequal opportunities for growth and development between the mates and wanting to insure against company embarrassment, corporations often gave wives the opportunity to take courses or to go to finishing school. Content was always directed and carefully controlled to preclude the possibility of such errant behavior as going into a business of her own!

A wife interviewed in 1958 drew a picture of manipulation that seems Orwellian today. After her husband had been subjected to a battery of aptitude and psychological tests as well as "depth" interviews, one hurdle remained—herself. She was required to write a letter indicating how willing (and happy) she would be to live in the place where he was to be assigned. She then related the agonies of the company-oriented social life—the artificiality of friendships that had to be based on "status rather than congeniality." Most oppressive was the lack of privacy in the company community, in which "Every purchase, every remark, every action was dissected over the telephone or the bridge table."[12] The social hierarchy reminded her of the army—where a family lived, what make of car it drove, what country club it belonged to were determined by executive rank.

It is particularly doubtful whether such "scientific" devices as psychological tests represent progress. They may add to alienation. There is an ethical issue in their use with prospective employees, let alone their wives. Do corporations have a moral right to mind-tap employees or their families? Shouldn't records, recommendations, interviews, and performance on the job suffice? Shouldn't the inner crevices of the mind be protected against intrusion by hired experts? Shouldn't a wife's potential paranoia or hysteria or mania remain beyond the reach of her husband's employer? It is true that employees or their wives are not *required* to undergo such testing. But reluctance here is all too often taken as evidence of incipient disease or, in more charitable circles, as a sign of uncooperativeness. A person's chances of being hired or promoted are vastly diminished if he resists these probings.

Richard Wytmar, a Chicago management counselor, sees a turn for the better in this regard. "There is an increasing awareness that companies can't fool around with a man and his wife as if they were pawns."[13] He attributes this improvement to changing social values and the influence of the younger generation's philosophy that everyone should do his own thing. Wytmar contends that the old practices are at last being seen as degrading and demeaning. Specifically companies are realizing that it is bad public relations to admit to screening and scrutinizing wives. And he credits Women's Liberation with giving women the courage to speak out and fight back.

But the screening and scrutinizing continues unabated, if unadmitted. With more subtlety than in the 1950s, the harassment, overt or threatened, is acutely felt by independent-minded wives, who resent being given the blame, but rarely the credit, for their husband's destiny. The techniques of snooping are now quite refined. In some instances the wife is invited to take psychological tests that are defined as aids in general personality adjustment for her own use as much as her husband's or the corporation's. She is then advised that she is no longer required to be docile and submissive. Should the findings show that she is aggressive and dominant, that is all to the good since it will indicate that she can be expected to run the household with a firm and determined hand, thereby freeing her husband from domestic worries and responsibilities. This is the way the company tries to destroy the impression that it demands the wife be a nonperson. Notice, however, that it still expects her to do the conventional thing—house management.

The company's expectations of what a spouse should do and be represent another aspect of corporate *machismo*. There are echoes of the military services here, as the wife interviewed in 1958 rightly detected. The armed forces wife must bow to the fact of life that what and who she is depends in great measure on her husband's rank. There is no pretense that she has a unique identity, an existence apart from her husband's. In the book *What Every Air Force Wife Should Know,* this point is made right in the author's preface. "You are the woman behind the man and while you are the silent partner, militarily speaking, your daily 'devotion to duty' sustains your husband as a valuable member of the United States Air Force."[14] Although the message might appall a humanist, this candor tells it like it is, without a dressing of euphemisms. And in a way the blunt method can be more reassuring psychologically than a mock-egalitarian preamble.

Similarly the book *What Every Army Wife Should Know* minces no words about wifely roles: "But wherever she lives an Army wife knows she has an important job. Like wives of many professional men, government officials, and some businessmen, she stands behind, as part of a 'team.' This is not to share in any part of his job but to give solid support in the home and socially." The army wife's role is crystal-clear. Under the heading "His Helpmate," she is told what her days are to be like: "Her husband and children, their well being and morale, their activities are her greatest concern."

What are described as "negative assets" of the army wife are not unlike those that executives feel about corporate wives. We learn: "These include not complaining when he has to work late, not discussing official matters unless they are for general knowledge, and not getting into controversy."

By and large corporate wives are still considered only in regard to their help to the corporation. Personal aspirations and needs as well as any spirit of independence are not only ignored but in most instances looked upon as encumbrances. In all the lists of what the good management wife should be that were sent by the 50 companies that I surveyed, although the words "cooperative," "gracious," and "accommodating" occur repetitively, never once does the word "intelligent" appear.

This viewpoint is taken not just by personnel staff but by executives themselves. In an article entitled "Executives, Wives—and Trouble," W. R. Roberts summarizes the answers to questions put to 300 top executives concerning their attitudes toward their own and other management wives.[15] The men were willing to respond, but Roberts notes that an interestingly large proportion (more than 60 percent) asked that their names not be used.

Anonymously then they all agreed that wives could cause serious trouble in the professional careers of their husbands as well as in the fortunes of even the largest corporation. The three commonest "sinners" among wives were the shrew who makes a man unhappy at home, the show-off who puts on the dog with other wives, and the aggressive vicarious climber who insists that her husband advance faster than his ability warrants. The respondents also frowned on the wife who discusses the important business of the organization, becomes too involved in company matters, is too outspoken or critical, or implies that she runs the company.

Although largely concurring about what the corporate wife should not do, the men showed no unanimity on what positive role she plays in the life of her husband or the corporation. Even those who would allow their names to be used were quite vague. Edward L. Steiniger, retired chairman of the board of Sinclair Oil Corporation, is quoted as saying that "Executives' wives are highly important." He believed they will become increasingly so because of expanding "social contacts among executives at dinners, clubs, charity affairs," and other occasions in mixed groups.

When asked what qualities make the perfect executive's wife, the responses singled out good manners, graciousness, and an even temper. Other attributes mentioned were attractiveness, skill as a conversationalist, friendliness, enthusiasm, unselfishness, and an interest in people. Some selected expressions of these executives were "a good dresser," "a patient sounding board for her husband," "acceptable to the community," "someone who entertains well," and "a good looker."

Similar to Whyte's findings in 1951, two-thirds of the executives felt it was necessary or highly desirable to meet the wife before the appointment of the husband to a new position. The principal reason for this was summarized by one executive thus: "When her qualities are an asset to her husband's career, this adds one more 'plus' to his rating and might bring about his selection over another man." This response is more diplomatically phrased than others, perhaps reflecting some misgivings about having placed too much emphasis on a wife's ability to undo her husband in the marketplace. Yet one executive boldly quoted Euripides: "Man's best possession is a sympathetic wife."

The two major problems that these executives noted concerning wives were moving and wives' accompanying husbands on trips. All agreed that maximum help should be extended to the wife in the moves that are necessary for the husband's work. Concerning the issue of taking her along on trips, there were both vagueness and a spectrum of opinion with very little consensus. One opinion was, "A wife should be included on a trip to a meeting or convention only if there is a planned program." Others responded, "She should go as often as she can be persuaded to do so."

An interesting hierarchical dilemma arose over the question of which wives should be allowed to come. At what level of management should wives accompany husbands on such trips? Here 38.2 percent stated that only wives of top management—of presidents, chairmen, and those listed as officers—be allowed to come; 32.4 percent broadened this to include senior management; and 29 percent would include wives of department heads and assistant vice-presidents. Taking wives along in all instances was predicated on the assumption that they would be cooperative and would add to and in no way detract from the business at hand. Regarding their own wives, the majority of these top executives—54 percent—had ambivalent feelings about taking them along; 9 percent never did while 37 percent did.

In all, the comments of the executives on what they thought of the wifely role would today be grist for any Women's Liberation mill. Their description of the ideal spouse fits that of the receptionist, secretary, or any subordinate employee. No one used the word "intelligent" or "independent" or "resourceful" in describing what a wife might be. The word "social" is mentioned—though with some trepidation. All agreed that she should have no part in any mind-using activities of the corporation. And it was quite evident that the wives really were not wanted at conventions and meetings.

In a report in 1968, a somewhat different response was found. Ninka Hart Burger quotes a representative of a large corporation disclaiming great concern about wives: "As long as the wife of any of our executives doesn't get her picture on the front page for murder or drunken driving, we don't care about her. It just doesn't matter."[16]

This "liberated" if cavalier attitude is exceptional, and it might have emanated from public relations consultants. Ms. Burger rightly observes that for hundreds of other American corporations, the executive wife does indeed matter, and for better or worse the recognition of her role is on the increase.

Whyte confirms this observation. There is the continued attitude, he reports, that the wife is the fly in the corporate ointment in that she remains somewhat outside of the social engineering that can be applied to her husband. Thus it was the lament of one top executive that "We control a man's environment in business and we lose it entirely when he crosses the threshold of his home." And "Management, therefore, has a challenge and an obligation to deliberately plan and create a favorable, constructive attitude on the part of the wife that will liberate her husband's total energies for the job."[17] How to achieve this total devotion remains baffling, though the legitimacy of such a goal is unquestioned.

No longer can the wife be forgotten as a passive object, obstacle, or annoyance but must be enlisted for corporate purposes. All corporate heads were in agreement that the ideal wife is to be highly adaptable, highly gregarious, and always aware that her husband belongs to the corporation.

But management now wants more than that; she is to have a more positive role, that of "social operator," and the best trait here is gregariousness. She must converse well without getting into controversy; she must "be able to put people at their ease." Some insurance companies attempt complete integration by actively promoting the wife (without separate pay) as part of a team. She is educated through periodicals on her role and psychological requirements. She is reminded that the contacts she makes through social and community activities might prove valuable in policy writing.

Although only a few corporations openly accept and promote this team concept, most exact a standard of conduct by wives that goes beyond cooperation. As "stabilizers" and "social operators," they must be assets to the corporation. One might say that it is partial integration—or put cynically, partial ownership of the wife.

THE GREAT WHYTE HOPE

An executive's wife should watch her figure and don't nag.

A FORD MOTOR COMPANY EXECUTIVE

In 1951 William H. Whyte, Jr., reported his findings on the state of the corporate wife of that time: ". . . among older executives there is a strong feeling that this younger generation of wives is the most cooperative the corporation has ever enlisted." Said one of his informants, "Somehow they seem to give us so much less trouble than the older ones." "Either the girls are better or the men are marrying better," said another. "But whatever it is with these people, they get along."[1]

Note that the most desirable attitudes a wife could have were to be "cooperative" and to "get along." And of course the new wives were referred to as having been "enlisted." The wife is clearly for corporation purposes; balkiness or independence of action are negative and undesirable qualities.

Whyte's executive interviewees were less than kind toward the older women, who, one must keep in mind, were their own wives. Apparently greener wives, like a neighbor's lawn, looked better. Whyte speculated about the fascination with the younger women. "Perhaps they have not grown older and more cantankerous." And he found "evidence that this group-mindedness is the result of a shift of values more profound than one might suppose. The change is by no means peculiar to the corporation wife, but by the nature of her job she may be the outstanding manifestation of it."

In writing of the wives as having jobs, corporation jobs that would be better done with the new spirit of group-mindedness, Whyte perhaps unwittingly expressed the executives' hope that the new breed of wife would eternally submerge her identity in her husband's and the corporation's. Two people for one salary—paycheck addressed to husband—for his and her lifetimes.

In a related article appearing the same year, Whyte reiterated his confidence that the coming generation of corporate wives would give management very little trouble.[2] As in the previous essay, he showed little concern about whether corporations would continue to give wives trouble. And with unflagging optimism he observed that American schools and colleges are turning out precisely the kind of wife corporate heads consider ideal, as Chapter 5 noted—the wife who realizes that her husband belongs to the corporation.[3]

Moreover, contrary to the fantasies of witch hunters, corporate wives do not seem to aspire to be the power behind the throne. Instead they see themselves as "negative" entities. Their value and importance reside in practical invisibility. They relate that the good wife does not complain when her husband comes home late from work, does not fuss when he is transferred, does not engage in controversial activities. Her role is one of stabilizer, refueler, or wailing wall. They agree as well that a good wife can't help her husband as much as a bad one—one who meddles, complains, or pushes—can hurt.

That a wife can hurt her husband's career is undeniable, at least in terms of the conventional corporate requirement that she lend herself devotedly to furthering it. There is the woman, for instance, who feels herself inadequate to meeting the demands of her corporation-assigned role and who hides her social anxieties by appearing arrogant and fearless. She appears as a know-it-all, tries to monopolize conversations, and hides her ignorance of the world by voicing strong opinions on subjects with little knowledge or understanding of them. When pressed for explanations or elucidations, she may fall back on "a woman's intuition" or resort to vituperative *ad hominem* remarks about the questioner. At the same time she affects a pseudo-charm meant to be ingratiating. As the wife of an executive with power, she can become vicious in influencing him to hire or fire people under him. Offending her can result in the ruination of innocent underlings. This woman frequently becomes frenetic in her desire to appear important and knowledgeable. Through her antics in the service of such needs, she can become an embarrassment to her husband and a threat to the corporation. There have been wives of our country's presidents and cabinet officers who are of this disposition. They are described by charitable friends as "eccentrics," by enemies as "mentally ill."

Unless her husband is sole owner of the company or unless he holds a majority of the corporation's shares, this wife's behavior causes so much turmoil that he may be forced to resign or be relegated to some remote nonsensitive area of the concern in a transfer amounting to semi-retirement. A pathetic figure, this woman is undone by having greatness thrust upon her. Because she never knows what to say, she talks all the time. Because she has never learned how to act properly, she mugs.

Because she longs for the simple life that she has been forced to leave, she pushes forward with grotesque relentlessness.

Equally—though perhaps not so publicly—damaging is the woman whose ambitions for her husband so outdistance his that she dismisses his best efforts as beneath her contempt, alienating him from their children and indeed from himself. This happens not uncommonly when a man marries "above his station"—a case we shall look at more closely in Chapter 8. With the "superior" wife, the rewards may be huge, but the husband had better not falter.

Before condemning such a woman as a horrible, castrating shrew, one must remember that if society provided the opportunities for the fulfillment of *her* considerable talents with a corresponding job or profession, she could reap the benefits of her own success (or the losses from her own failure) instead of latching vampire fashion on to her hapless mate's. It is the height of folly to believe that because women are "feminine" they are not ambitious. Because of their training in modesty, women rarely if ever present themselves as Lady Macbeths. Throughout history they have been used as scapegoats, blamed for the sins of others: men. Very often a man's excessive ambition or financial conniving is attributed to pressure from his wife. And it is indeed true that wives interested in promoting gains for their families and wanting compensation in a material way for the deprivations and renunciations they have had to suffer in their own existence often become unsubtle in their expressions and tactics.

Yet do they deserve the condemnation that is glibly heaped on them? Under the gratuitously uncharitable rubric of "Family Baggage," Robert Townsend writes: "The worst wives (from the standpoint of the effect on their husbands) in my experience are the overly ambitious ones. They seem constantly after their husbands to make more money. They don't understand that money, like prestige, if sought directly, is almost never gained. It must come as a byproduct of some worthwhile objective or result which is sought and achieved for its own sake."[4]

Although Townsend might defend himself by saying that he was only advising the corporate wife to be more tactful and less obvious, the tone of his admonition is fairly typical of sexism. Why is the woman denounced for being candid about the urge to succeed which is so lauded when it comes from a man? After all isn't the name of the game acquisition? We heap nothing but praise and admiration on the executive who votes himself extra bonuses, stock options, and generous pension plans. But woe to the woman who gives the appearance of pushing her husband. Here again is the double standard that colors so much of our thinking about how men and women should behave.

This is a way men have of continuing to think well of one another by blaming untoward reactions and behavior on the female influence—a holdover from the days of the Inquisition and before, when it was generally assumed that it was the woman who brought evil into the world and who was the principal cause of discord among men. For their purported villainies, women were tortured and killed as witches by their fathers, husbands, and brothers for more than 700 years. Are we sure that these fanatical suspicions have been laid to rest with the last burning?

Perhaps many corporate wives are taking no chances. Sherry Baltimore, 30 years old, is a busy corporate wife who fills in when her husband's secretary is on vacation, travels with her husband on business, helps him entertain customers, and talks with him about his work even when she is bored. Although it is hard to quantify such contributions, it must be pointed out that her husband, Richard, a Formica salesman for the American Cyanamid Company, recently won the Golden Oval award from his company for exceptional salesmanship—for the second time.

Cyanamid has 2,000 salesmen and saleswomen, but all the Golden Oval winners are male. Perhaps the 30 or 40 women do not sell as well because they don't have wives to help them in their careers.

And the wives do indeed see that as their role.[5] None of the Golden Oval winners' wives interviewed has an outside job. Most of them spend a considerable amount of time helping their husbands with sales work and their lives are geared to making their husbands' careers a success. "The company sees its men as a tremendous asset, and their wives as a prime-mover in the success of that asset. Thus, the wives play an indirect role in the success of the company," said Roy Schenberg, Cyanamid's manager of press relations.

What are the challenges and opportunities for growth for the corporate wife, what her rewards? Whatever the hardships for the corporate husband, and there are many, as Miles Duley's letter confirmed, he at least experiences the excitement of involvement. For him there is a chance to grow, and whether he succeeds or fails, he has had the opportunity to use his mind and wits. Only exceptionally is this the case for the corporate wife. Only rarely are the rewards in personal development commensurate with the attrition to which she is exposed. It is wishful thinking, Mr. Duley, to say or hope that the woman who needs "status and recognition" in her own right is an isolated instance. I fear that invoking the simple virtues of "maturity" and "objectivity" to solve such complex problems has the motive of shoving wives into cooperating.

The time-honored male prerogative of working, with its growth-producing challenges and associations, is the best way of literally keeping one's sanity. We have this from no less an authority than Sigmund Freud, the father of psychoanalysis:

> No other technique for the conduct of life attaches the individual so firmly to reality as laying emphasis on work: for his work at least gives him a secure place in a portion of reality, in the human community. The possibility it offers of displacing a large amount of libidinal components, whether narcissistic, aggressive or even erotic, on to professional work and on to the human relations connected with it lends it a value by no means second to what it enjoys as something indispensable to the preservation and justification of existence in society.[6]

Does this apply to the corporate wife as well? How is she to test reality in the human community? And on whom is she to displace "libidinal components"? Freud's statement adroitly defines the role of work in keeping one's identity, integrity, and yes, sanity. One might add that it is also a great antidote for loneliness. It is a valid and salutary prescription, if not an imperative, for both sexes. Until now, however, the corporate wife has been largely deprived of this "technique."

Wives have learned from life and from their mothers that their own destinies and those of their children depend almost solely on how well their husbands do. Because the world has made them clinging vines, they soon learn that climbing is basic. They therefore do everything they can, using their personal charm and past education as well as personal community work, to promote their husband-candidate up the ladder. To do less would be self-defeating.

It was an old story in the royal courts of Europe that a woman who became a favorite of the king could do much for her husband. And husbands have been known to tolerate even a wife's infidelity when a promotion accrued. In Shakespeare's *Othello* Emilia, Iago's wife, tells the unbelieving, ingenuous Desdemona, "Why, who would not make her husband a cuckold to make him a monarch? I should venture purgatory for it." Modern life is too sophisticated for such direct approaches to success, but wives of junior executives operate subtler means to power daily. There are twentieth-century Emilias who know that ingratiating themselves in the executive suite often brings grand rewards for their husbands. The ingratiation is usually not directly sexual but of a nature that enhances and flatters the ego of the upper managers. The wife shows her loyalty in her willingness to make difficult moves without rancor, in her ability to entertain important customers with grace and charm, and in her renunciations of all interests other than those consonant with corporate wifely duties. In short, although it is frequently said of the man that he is married to his work or business, it is closer to the mark to say that it is the young wife of the future Mr. Success who must marry his corporation.

What of the woman who combines a job of her own with homemaking? Does this not give her a certain independence? Usually not. A personal survey of women recently married found that the great majority would gladly move anywhere their husbands could get a good job. Many of these young women worked, often at lowly jobs, so that their mates could complete their education. They understandably didn't want their own considerable labors and investment to go for naught.

There can be no criticism of these young people who want a part of the American dream. In the first instance economic power eclipses all others as one strives to get a foot on the ladder of success—no time here for the abstract niceties of living in the form of an independent career for the young woman. She can have no concern for Women's Liberation or identity problems, because realistically she knows that it is through the man and only through the man that her family is apt to achieve financial success. The job of typist, secretary, or filing clerk that she held while her husband went to college was no launching pad for her for bigger and better things. In 20 years she might be chief typist. Smart and perceptive as she is, she puts her money on the male, to whom society has given special advantage over women in the pursuit of worldly goals. For these young women the concepts of equality for the sexes—equal rights and opportunity, nondiscriminatory hiring practices, and the companionate model of marriage—are pie-in-the sky ideas that appear not only unrelated to their problems but completely inimical to their well-being. What happens later on, as indicated in the case history in the Prologue, is another story. And it would be pure foolishness to advise these young women to act against their homing instincts. Their intuitive appraisals are sadly correct: for a young woman, as feminist Gloria Steinem and others have observed, union with a young man of potential is probably the only avenue open for social and economic elevation unless she was born of an influential (and doting) father.

As time goes by, money begins to take on other meanings in the marriage, meanings derived from the fact that it is a commodity the male of the species comes by more readily than can the female. Because money does mean power, it enters into the battle of the sexes. Men who are unable to give of themselves because of the pressures and demands of their corporate or public lives try to buy peace via the checkbook from their wives' complaints of boredom, loneliness, or spiritual abandonment. In its way it works. For in the crunch he has earned the rejoinder, "Haven't I always given you everything?" or "You've done pretty well for yourself for a girl from a little mining town in the West!"

Women learn from the cradle that direct confrontation over their complaints is doomed to failure when they are economically dependent. This is perhaps the reason for the appearance of hysteria, occurring predominantly in women. Hysteria is an implement of a need to protest that cannot be expressed openly. Unless men realize that there is this underlying struggle going on, they are left asking the naive question, "What did I do wrong?" They are heirs to an inglorious historical tradition that degrades and persecutes their mothers, sisters, wives, and daughters. They should not be shocked when their own "generosity" and "altruism" bring forth the paradoxical response of negativism, withdrawal, or emotional outburst.

The economic power that women gain through men's success must substitute for a lifetime of inequities. Only because of biological longevity does a wife stand a chance of commanding this power herself. She may inherit a great deal of it and live to see her sons ascend to heights often beyond her husband's. If she is lucky she may for the first time use it for her own purposes and causes—although many a corporate husband sets up a trust for his wife or otherwise makes sure her control over wealth is well-guarded by male managers, bankers, or stockbrokers.

Perhaps these thoughts of ultimate power help alleviate the pains of loneliness and the host of humiliations that corporate wives suffer. While it may not be strictly true that the meek shall inherit the earth, for women inheriting has been the only way.

The imperative of financial security is unassailable, but as someone purportedly said, "Man *and woman* do not live by bread alone." The myth that one can has led to horrible disillusionment. We are distinguished from the rest of the animal kingdom by having minds and, it is hoped, minds of our own. Having a mind entails involvement with others, with our environment and community. Human beings quickly deteriorate when they live solipsistically. Without community involvement and concern, without the feeling of having some say about one's own destiny, without the opportunity for meaningful and effective participation in civic affairs and communal institutions, one is reduced to a shell, a state so many of us reach after twenty or thirty years of atrophy due to disuse of mental capacities. I am appalled when I hear young women say, as I do all too often, "I want to get married so that my husband can make all the decisions. I do hate making decisions." There is something horribly wrong with the way we bring up our daughters if at the age of 20 a young woman can volunteer such a statement and, most sadly, with a sense of pride as if she is being properly "feminine." Would we not be contemptuous of any other American who would acclaim with pride that he wants to be run and indeed run over?

An acid truth that women and men are beginning to face only today is that denigration of the female is built into our culture. She is expected to forfeit the human need for individuality, to submerge her destiny in the lives of the men she depends on. Carrying the conviction of her own lack of worth, she needs great strength of character to wrest personal recognition from those in power—the men in her life. Woe betide her if those men are more than ordinarily overbearing, as in the following case history. This example of the suppression of the dignity of another illustrates the particular hazard of being the wife of an authority figure in our culture, in this instance a physician.

The patient was a 44-year-old woman who came into treatment because of feelings of despondency and fear that she was "losing her mind." She related that she seemed to be in a constant state of tearfulness and to have lost her ability to control her emotions. She lacked any confidence in running her household and in dealing with the problems of her children. Because she doubted her sanity, she felt that she could not advise her children or discipline them with any assurance that she was acting wisely. She began to drink quite heavily from the amply-stocked liquor cabinet.

The second of four children, she had grown up in a rural area where her father had been the country doctor. He had worked hard at his practice, but the family had always seemed to be in difficult financial circumstances. Physical illness had made it impossible for him to work during the last 15 years of his life. She described him as kind and just, but "We all knew it when Father was in the house." She described her mother as very passive and placid, with little formal education. Her life had been devoted to keeping the household in an orderly fashion so that the father would not be offended. Her mother's needs had been minimal; the patient recalled that she had rarely left the house. The mother had visited neither friends nor relatives, feeling that she should always be around when her husband needed her. She had kept up contact with the outside world largely through letter writing, an occupation that had taken up all her spare time. She had seemed happy, with no apparent need for any personal distinction.

The patient's life was overtly conventional; she had graduated from high school and gone to college for several years, which had trained her for a professional job. She had worked, supporting herself and gaining some distinction in her field. At the age of 28, she had married her husband, who was already a successful obstetrician in his community. He had been married before this. For the first few years her marriage had been a happy one, but with the advent of children (she now had four), she became increasingly oppressed by the loneliness and tediousness of what she called "the life of being a lady in waiting," which is the fate of an obstetrician's wife. As the children made increasing demands on her time and energy, she felt more and more discontented with her role. Her husband could not understand any reason for her discontentment. Didn't he provide everything she wanted? He criticized her for not caring for the household and the children more efficiently, with all the "spare time" she had. On the other hand he bitterly resented any public activities that she might embark on independently; he wanted her to participate only in activities that were associated with his own, such as medical auxiliary or nurse's aide work. He could not understand that she did not derive gratification from his many successes as both a physician and a community leader.

One of her husband's chief interests was mental health, which he promoted and worked for in his community. He was a psychiatry buff and had great respect for the psychiatric and psychosomatic approaches to medical problems. However, he was very self-righteous about his own conduct and looked on his success as proof of his inner strength and obvious normality. As the patient increasingly lost interest in the activities that were important to him and as he was reluctant to recognize any personal interests that she might develop, there were many altercations and struggles. He informed her that anyone who could not be happy in the situation he had provided obviously had something radically wrong with her.

One of his motives for promoting mental health organizations in the community was to provide aid for his wife. After one bitter quarrel, he made an appointment for her with an internist, a confrere of his. He wanted a thorough examination made, including blood sugar tests and other metabolic studies to rule out a physical cause of her terrible disposition and unreasonableness. She was reluctant to go for the examination, but since he had made the appointment, she did not want to cause general embarrassment. She was found to be in perfect health, although at the time the internist also "assured" her that he would give a complete report to her husband. When she questioned her husband about the report, he was ambiguous.

The situation between them continued to deteriorate and at a faster rate now, so the husband sought the help of a new psychiatrist in the community, one over whom he had much political control. She saw this specialist a dozen times, but the transaction proved to be a fiasco because of the frequent inquiries made by the husband. The psychiatrist was apparently too politically involved to be able to resist.

The patient became hopeless about her plight. She now had increasing difficulty dealing with the children and thought of sending the older two away from home.

I received a phone call from her husband asking for an appointment for her. I explained that it is my policy to refuse any requests for psychiatric consultation that do not come from the person involved. He could not understand this but said that he would try to get his wife to call for an appointment. A few weeks later she did call. After several interviews she decided to go into psychotherapy.

Even though the arrangements were made privately with the patient, she had the feeling that I was an agent of her husband. And indeed on several occasions, directly or indirectly, he attempted to get information. When he realized he could not control the psychotherapeutic situation, he was outraged and demanded that she quit. (He told her, "Until you can do things the way I want them done, I can't consider you a normal person.") Despite this the patient continued therapy, which proved to be quite successful for her. She quit drinking and regained her role in the household, and her tearfulness ended. The couple was gradually able to argue about the differences in feelings and opinions that may exist between two people without one's being abnormal. There is little happiness here for either of them, but considerably more dignity has entered the relationship.

This case history demonstrates the very special type of power that a physician has and that he can often wield in his family. This is probably even truer in the home of a psychiatrist or psychologist. Judging behavior and giving opinions on what is normal or abnormal can have far-reaching and devastating effects, especially when the judge is a so-called specialist. It can lead to tyranny through such threatening attacks as "If you do not agree with me, you must be abnormal—or crazy." The specter of the mental hospital is also present. The physician can also use the power of his relationships with confreres, who may be beholden to him in both professional and political ways. The feeling of conspiracy that the mate might have would not in any sense be delusional.

Overbearing people have a way of doing all but the right things. They confuse the needs of the person they purportedly want to help with their own. Used to giving orders and being obeyed by people who have no alternative, they begin to overvalue both their own importance and their wisdom. How angry this important person then becomes when things and wives go awry! And sadly there are enough "experts"—physicians, psychiatrists, and psychologists—themselves brought up to be in awe of power, to validate the "great" man's arrogance by cooperating in the future diminution of his victims.

Being the "enlisted" person does not suffice for any woman, and her distress mounts as she grows older. The mature wife had best not want a career of her own—it is much too late for that in most instances. Studies show that she appears to want only more attention and togetherness, which can never come, for she cannot compete for her husband's interest against the excitement, challenge, and gratifications that go with professional status. Men in America band together in all their important work and play; women are poorly tolerated in anything but subservient roles. The wife is not to be part of any high-level decision-making group but is expected merely to be cooperative in helping her husband.

For many a corporate wife, the more she cooperates, the less he can be with her. It is understandable then that she might feel she had cooperated in the mechanism leading to her own undoing. It is just possible that 20 years of subservience with ever-diminishing meaningful rewards might lead to unhappiness no matter how buoyant the initial spirit. People forget that "cooperativeness" is not a self-energizing virtue, even for the dutiful wives of corporate America.

The dutiful young wives described by Whyte in 1951 had in fact already begun to display some cantankerousness by 1958. In that year an article entitled "I Hate My Husband's Success" reported an interview by Alice Lake of a corporate wife who said angrily, "The company tells me what to wear and read. It decides the opinions I can express in public. It even picks my dinner guests." She told of complaints that did not originate with her but were representative of thousands of other women who "are imprisoned in company-imposed conformity": "We must belong to a team—be part of the big company family. . . . A man's promotion may depend on whether his wife meets the approval of the president's wife." The article ends with the following:

> Bill loves his job. Because he shares common business interests with our guests, he does not bore easily during these pseudosocial evenings. The exhilaration of clinching a contract or developing a deal pays him for the interminable chitchat of the cocktail party.
>
> I am paid neither in job satisfaction nor in cash for my work. I did not choose the job of executive wife, and I am heartily sick of it.
>
> I know that there are still corporations which purchase a man's talents without hiring his wife. We recently had dinner with the personnel manager of such a company. "If a man's fitted for his job," he told me, "we're reasonably certain he's chosen a wife who's qualified

for hers. Her job at home doesn't concern us, and we just don't inquire into it."

I do not believe it is necessary for the wife of an executive to marry the company in order to have her husband succeed. I'm ready to start a revolution to divorce the home from the office.

Anyone want to join?"

A challenging invitation from an obviously vigorous—and exceptionally determined—young woman. Few of her contemporaries, however, heeded her call; it took another decade for great numbers of them even to contemplate joining the movement for the liberation of women. Most wives in their late 20s or early 30s have not reached the point of desperation that often drives their older sisters to revolt. Those who have may express their distress not in overt rebellion but in the covert resistance that surfaces as "neurosis."

Take the case of a simple, timid 28-year-old housewife who was referred to me for psychotherapy by her family physician after she failed to respond to a variety of tranquilizers and other psychotropic drugs. Her presenting symptoms were episodes of severe apprehension in the street and in stores, fear that she might harm her 3-year-old daughter, and—as with the doctor's wife—fear of losing her mind. She was a plain-looking woman who had had little formal education, and she showed all the signs of social bewilderment and ineptness. The theory that she was beset with imaginary dangers stemming from drives from within was only part of the story.

The patient related that she was the elder of two children, having a brother five years younger than she. Her parents had immigrated from Eastern Europe and were of the Russian Orthodox religion. Her father had advanced to a semimanagerial position in a small, paternalistic company. Her mother had worked periodically to supplement the family income. The patient had been brought up under strict discipline. She had been a docile child and adolescent, giving proper obedience and respect to her parents. Her father had worried about her outside activities and fretted about some of her girl friends. He had often followed her to school and met her on her return to see that she did not stray into "corrupting" circles of teenagers. Her social life had therefore been restricted, but she had managed to have some friends of both sexes. She had never evidenced any rebelliousness.

After high school no mention had been made of further education though she had done fairly well in her courses. Instead her father had gotten her a job as a stenographer with his company. (Nepotism went along with the paternalism of this concern.) He had prided himself on being able to place his daughter in a secure setting where he could keep his eye on her. She had not been consulted on where she would like to work or at what; it had been assumed that any girl would be grateful for such a job.

At work, again through her father, she had met a young college student who worked there during the summer while preparing to become an engineer. Her father had thought of this as a fine match and had done everything to encourage the relationship. When the young man had completed college, he and she had married, and he had returned to the same company as a full-time employee. After her marriage she had left her job, and a daughter had been born soon thereafter. The external circumstances of her life appeared ideal—she had a husband who was good to her and who had a bright future, satisfied parents, a nice home, and a healthy baby.

Concurrently her younger brother had been approaching manhood. The course of his life, however, contrasted sharply with hers. An inferior student in high school, he had nonetheless been encouraged to go to college. He had been fully supported financially and even given a car when transportation had become a problem. With some continuing academic difficulties, he had completed college and had immediately been hired by an architectural firm at a good starting salary. There had been no suggestion that he join the father's company, which was thought to give inadequate opportunity for his talents.

Three years after the birth of her daughter, the patient responded to her seemingly ideal external conditions with the symptoms mentioned earlier. This was a puzzle to everyone and a cause of rage to her father, who did not want his daughter to be a burden to his son-in-law. The patient found no friendly listener among her relatives—they interpreted her sadness and fearfulness as signs of selfishness and ingratitude. "Doesn't she have everything? What more does she want?"

Yet she was beset with attacks of anxiety. "I'm afraid something is going to happen, but I don't know what it is," she said.

What had she to fear? She was accepted by her friends and family, loved by her husband, seemingly fulfilled as a woman and mother. There were certainly no external dangers; she probably had more security than the average person. Internal dangers of course might include fear of sexual feelings, long repressed or contaminated by earlier parental threats and warnings. Then there was the fear of harming her daughter, an obsessive thought that might too readily be interpreted as sadistic in quality. Clearly her anxiety could be seen as a reaction to danger from within, there being "none" from without.

However, the hypothesis that proved to be most logical and enlightening was that her anxiety was a response of anticipation to future dangers that were as much outside herself as within. This encompassed her life style, which she saw as set for the next 30 or 40 years. She would continue to be dutiful and obedient, now to her husband instead of to parents; there would appear neither choices nor challenges—she would live an uninterrupted continuation of the first 20 years of her life.

As her life story unfolded, it became apparent that her timidity and docility had naturally deprived her of adventuresomeness, choice-making ability, and even minimal self-determination. We soon became aware that in her apprehensive exclamation, "I'm afraid something is going to happen, but I don't know what it is," she was secretly lamenting the danger that indeed *the opposite* would be true—that in her life *nothing* would happen. She had been caught in a secure trap with no courage to complain or to extricate herself. Her life at home, in the streets, and in the stores was devoid of deprivation, predatory human beings, or ferocious animals. The absence of challenge, of decision making, of problem solving would instead be her destiny. Even her daughter at the age of 3 appeared self-sufficient, engaging only a small part of her time and attention.

The contrasting fate of her brother proved to be an aggravating factor in this woman's condition. This was no neurotic sibling rivalry but a realistic, objective appraisal of the inequities attending the raising of a son and daughter in a family of this socioeconomic stratum, where the son is held to be a dividend but the daughter a mortgage. Credit for intelligence, judgment, choice making, and self-determination was lavished on the son but never was accorded the daughter. Not one to complain, she nonetheless felt the inequity and responded to it with her cryptic alarm and protest.

Then of course the contrasting life of her husband, who eclipsed her in all facets of life, added to her sense of inferiority and inadequacy. As he progressed in his work and associations, they were hardly able to speak the same language. Yet he never expressed irritation or annoyance. She was expected only to play her wifely biological role and remain unobtrusive. Absorbed in his interesting work, he had little concern for her growth.

Similarly her untoward thoughts about her daughter originated in her chagrin over the fate of the female. Was her daughter to be destroyed as she thought herself to be? Would destiny impel her to foist on her daughter the inequities she herself felt?

These are real dangers, and they are external, but they may not be immediately apparent. One is not justified in declaring them either unreal or internal because they are not universally perceived or acknowledged.

The course of psychotherapy was in large measure predictable. For a long period she both affirmed and disclaimed her boredom, her dissatisfaction, and her own social insignificance. She asked the questions put to her by her husband, her parents, and her own superego. Why she? Why was everyone else in her circumstances contented with life? No one else had to go to a doctor! And when would she stop going? Was she really indulging herself in receiving a "talking" treatment? Was she in truth going through an infatuation with the doctor when she should have her mind on her family and household chores? The area of greatest suspicion was the absence of medication in therapy. There are now miracle drugs that bring contentment. The doctor seemed to be agitating rather than relieving. The husband began contemplating what might happen to the marriage. He felt predictably that she must "change her attitude," and then all would be well. In this there was inordinate pressure for chemical tranquilization so that she would no longer be a disrupting factor.

With insights she began observing and noting that all was not so tranquil with others "in her circumstances." It became a source of pride for her to recognize new aspects of living and forces that were acting on her and others. When she finally became aware of her legitimate struggle against nothingness, her physical symptoms largely abated, and her energies were channeled into areas that might change her plight. This eventually was encouraging to the husband, who earlier had felt he was at the end of his rope in dealing with her and had wondered whether she should be hospitalized.

Was her past disturbing? Yes. In her early years her parents had been in the throes of elevating themselves from the poverty level of existence. Both had worked hard, and there had always been anxiety lest the fragile progress be impeded. The children had had to be well-disciplined and separated from the temptations that might bring social disaster. The father had never departed from the proper behavior and decorum his boss demanded. At times it had been touch and go, but gradually he had become a member of the team and felt a modicum of security. Overhanging his existence, however, was his lack of formal education; he had felt pressure from new employees, by then almost entirely college-trained. Here he had been confronted with his ambivalence toward education. On the one hand determined that his own son would receive "the best education possible," conscious as he was of his own deficiencies vis-à-vis the upcoming young men "who could write a decent letter when they had to," on the other his pride could not have allowed his daughter to have more education than he had. In this time of life, as if learning from Lear, he would not have a daughter lording it over him. His frustrations had been unevenly distributed, focusing on the female as is typical. For him a girl was a success if she caused no trouble or disgrace, as through becoming a "bum" or getting pregnant out of wedlock. He had heard that girls who went off to college were apt to go wild, losing respect for parents and bringing shame to the family name. It would not do for his son to have a sister who was a tramp. Elevation to the middle class had come hard enough; there was no need for experimentation.

She had become Daddy's girl and had frequently been the only one in the family who could talk back to him, though only in inconsequential areas. She had been very solicitous of her brother, seeking to protect him from the wrath of their father on the infrequent occasions when he had been rebellious. Toward her mother she had been similarly solicitous but had felt neither awe nor affection.

In her teens the sexual threat, the specter of going wrong, had been constant and had made sex loathsome, mysterious, and intriguing. Her one great power was to undo; her father had made her aware of this. At times his very preoccupation with sex had appeared to her as a command. She had felt he was almost disppointed, she related, that she was not adventuresome in this area. Sexual adjustment in marriage after the initial shock had been satisfactory to both spouses and remained so. When she had married, the family, particularly her father, breathed a sigh of relief; the ordeal of carrying a daughter through the pitfalls of adolescence had ended in success.

But her obsequiousness was more apparent than real. Unexpectedly she became aware that she was paying too high a price for others' needs, real or fancied. Her neurosis, developing as it did, was her rebellion. She was not spoiled by success, as some would say. Instead she sought to save herself from complete annihilation by a self-preserving negativism, a refusal to become the possession and vassal of still another man (her husband) who would take her for granted.

With her training and timidity, she could not become an aggressive woman to show her protest. What was left to her was more of the same: to exaggerate her timidity to a fault, literally to become afraid of her own shadow (how much more "feminine" and passive can one get?). In effect she was anticipating her own social and psychological death. Luckily she was concerned about her destiny and cried out against its seeming inevitability. Her anxiety was salutary and self-preserving; she would "not go gentle into that good night."

The patient's symptoms allowed her to separate herself from the fate of the young women with whom she had grown up and who now surrounded her in the suburbs. She withdrew from the role of shopper and beauty parlor captive. In her home she held her ground in having but one child, no minor feat in light of persistent pressure from her husband ("Don't you love me?"), relatives, friends, and the church.

Limited by lack of education and worldly experience, she had only modest positive accomplishments. She was able to work part time as a door-to-door canvasser for a research corporation. This was surely not world-shaking, but it nonetheless dismayed and puzzled her relatives, who deemed such work dangerous for a woman, especially since it brought her into the inner city. Plagued by anxiety in supermarkets and beauty salons, she experienced no fears in this outside work but only exhilaration, giving evidence once again that the overriding danger to her existence lay in the "safety" of the housewife's role. The hostile elements in her environment were not the people of the street but her "loved" ones, who saw her as pure biology.

Therapy encouraged her to carry out her worldly aspirations. A woman's destiny might indeed be broadened. As a result she began to feel human and rational, contrary to the sense of herself she had brought into treatment: in her milieu she had been perceived as insane at best, misanthropic at worst. Incidentally she had a fortuitous assist from the fast-moving events of the world. With the new urgency for population control, her insistence on not having more children now appeared as not entirely nonsensical and selfish to some around her.

Attuned as we are to the threats of nefarious drives from within and catastrophic events from without, we may forget the despair that comes from the prospect of a passionless and unchallenging existence. The trauma of eventlessness, of nothing at all ever happening, can be a catastrophe of major proportions. Such was the threat to the patient just described. Foreseeing no escape from the emptiness of her existence, she affected a caricature of the feminine role of timidity and docility. She would be a housewife to a fault. So devoted to the home would she be that she would not set foot outside it. She could therefore never be tempted by worldly excitements. She literally left the outside world to her successful corporate husband. At the same time, again through her symptoms, she gave messages of protest and concern over disappearing into the wallpaper.

People do this unconsciously through illness when they are blocked by a thicket of reasons from being able to articulate their discontentment through the usual channels. Among these reasons is the general societal intolerance of a woman's rejection of her traditional role. One then tries to communicate as well as one can through the cryptography of a neurosis.

Other things being equal, however, the discontentment will ultimately out in clear-cut dissent. Alice Lake's interviewee said wryly that she was "ready to start a revolution." And while the call to arms has not escalated into open warfare, it has sounded echoing disgruntlement among the women—now 20 years older—whom Whyte saw in 1951 as a new and cooperative breed.

Lois Wyse has reexamined those new and other corporate wives in her book *Mrs. Success*.[8] The "group minded" women of Whyte's survey *have* become cantankerous, at least as discontented with their lot in life as the previous generation. Ms. Wyse indicates that the most dissatisfied wives are those married to chief executive officers. Those married to junior executives seem less unhappy. The unhappiness of the wife seems to be in direct proportion to the success of her man. Nonetheless her personal identity remains secondary to that of her husband and the corporation. Only 16 percent of the women expressed a longing for a career of their own; nearly 50 percent had no desire for a career even though a majority have earned a bachelor's degree. They are housewives, cooking and cleaning as well as supervising help. Their discontent seems to be based not on the lack of an identity of their own but on the absence from home of their successful husbands

From Lois Wyse's data it is quite apparent that most corporate wives are conventional in their overt responses. Yet they are unhappy and cantankerous; despite some exceptions corporate living apparently does not gratify them as it does their husbands.

Interesting also is the apparent dissatisfaction with their personal lives shown by executive wives who claim to be happy. In an article entitled "For These Women, Marriage Is Enough," Enid Nemy reports on interviews with the wives of three top American executives.[9] Each indicated that she is happy in her role of gearing herself to her husband's life. These women make the best of the moments they and their husbands have together and hold themselves ready to accompany them whenever possible, but they are not without complaints. "Anything else I do is sandwiched-in time. Most of the corporation wives I know lead our lives in the shadow of our husbands but I don't think we lose our identity." What for some might appear to be a flagrant lack of communication or trust is apparently a source of pride for one wife: "I adore being around business men and women . . . they are much more intriguing to me than the jet set or artists . . . but my husband never discusses business with me."

Finally, another corporate wife, a mother of seven, describes what her husband expects her to be: ". . . useful, punctual, efficient, pleasant, alert and healthy. He has no patience with the opposite of these. He wants me to be feminine, to have a sense of humor without being witty and not to be emphatic. I have learned quickly to compromise."

In a related article on the same page with the title ". . . But Some Company Wives Hear Echoes of Women's Liberation," Agis Salpukas begins by quoting an executive wife who said: "I bask in my husband's reflected glory. I don't have to be anything myself. His status is my status. Sometimes I feel he's living his life to the fullest and I'm living his life to the fullest." Some of the women interviewed noted that their husbands said they felt threatened when they began to carve out careers for themselves. "They've been taking care of you and then you show them that you can take care of yourself."

Reporter Salpukas found some though not much dissension at a conference of corporate wives in Detroit sponsored by the Division of Continuing Education at Oakland University. Here women whose husbands were for the most part in middle management but in the income bracket above $25,000 a year voiced sentiments about identity needs apart from those of wife and mother. They admitted to being affected by Women's Liberation, and some had plans for returning for further education and pursuing personal careers. However, it was evident that "Most of the women were in no mood to challenge traditional assumptions about themselves." There was little or no objection when a Ford Motor Company executive told them that if the corporate wife wanted outside interests, "She should take painting, music, go to school but under no circumstances take a job." He then added that an executive's wife should "watch her figure and don't nag."

Intriguingly enough, his advice would raise a protest from none other than that commentator on the "cooperative" wife, William H. Whyte, Jr. In the final section, called "In Praise of the Ornery Wife," he embarks on an issue that has rarely if ever been mentioned or pondered in the literature on corporation wives: whether adjustment and adaptability may prove to be counterproductive to corporate goals. We have focused, Whyte points out, on "the well-adjusted group" to furnish our creative power. This is fine, but he goes on most perceptively to say: "It is equally true, however, that a real advance in a field inevitably involves a conflict with the environment. And unless people temper their worship of environment, they may well evoke a society so well adjusted that no one would be able—or willing—to give it the sort of hotfoot it regularly needs."[10]

THE ANATOMY
OF LONELINESS

All men's misfortunes spring from their hatred of being alone.

JEAN DE LA BRUYÈRE

ALL COMMENTATORS on the corporate wife seem to agree that her principal disease is loneliness. And yet this may not be an endemic but an epidemic illness, contagious in every segment of society.

We learn that corporate men are lonely, both in their travels and in their offices. Caught up in what David Riesman has called the "antagonistic" cooperation of big business, they secretly yearn for more trust and genuine friendship, which are absent both from competitors on the outside and inside the organization. Security is always relative: one bad step and everything can be lost. One must maintain a front of confidence and mastery lest someone detect a hidden weakness or deficiency. Despite his success, there is no one such a man can confide in concerning the vital issues that may plague him. He never knows when some conversation or memo may be used against him. Ultimately he must keep his own counsel; he may not talk about certain matters even with his wife, for she might inadvertently betray him. This obviously leads to isolation and loneliness.

This life style contributes to the anger and disappointment corporate men feel when they come home at night to an unsympathetic wife and family who are seemingly enmeshed in trivial household problems. The corporate husband is continually lamenting, "She just doesn't realize what I go through all day," or "Doesn't a man deserve a few hours of peace in his life?" He is responding to the real fears and dangers of his existence and longs for some uncensorious relationship. He is certainly in no condition to receive more of the same when he arrives home.

Yet *his* experience of loneliness is mitigated by the compensations of challenge and growth that are also an integral part of his work. His personal isolation, certainly painful, is largely relieved by the balm of success, challenge, and achievement. For the corporate wife these compensatory mechanisms are not there. She is much more vulnerable and therefore feels the effects of isolation and estrangement more intensely. There is no comparable balm for her injury.

We have already spoken of the difficulties for the wife of transferring her credentials. We have already alluded to the great scrutiny she is under and the pitifully small rewards that accrue to her. We have already mentioned the almost automatic blame, like that heaped on the "witches" of old, that falls on her if she steps out of line even minimally. We will document in Chapter 8 the flagrant double standard in sexual matters that combines with inequities in a hundred other areas to cause her frustration and deprivation. This is clearly not my personal observation only. Besides the increasing number of corporate wives (and daughters) who are reaching the consultation rooms of psychiatrists and the wards of mental hospitals, each succeeding book and article on the subject is uniformly cacophonous.

Loneliness for the corporate wife is of course far more than being separated from the "great" man. It means being separated from those resources of culture, community, and people that make up a human existence. Loneliness means being left behind in knowledge, participation, mental growth, and influence. When one hears a wife lament, "He couldn't take me along," or "I have to stay behind with the children," it literally means she has been left out of the opportunity for liberation and growth. And without growth there is stagnation and death. Deaths can be many; the biological is but one. People worry rightly about their professional, social, and political as well as their biological survival.

To be cut off from communication with other human beings is to feel lonely. But more important, to be out of touch with parts of one's inner self is to feel lonely. This includes the diminution or loss of previously developed talents and interests—the dancing one enjoyed, the music one played, the writing one did. It means the loss of one's skills as an artist, a teacher, or a technician. To be separated from these parts of one's being, these implements of past participation and gratification, contributes to an especially adverse type of loneliness. Erich Kahler writes, "The estrangement between human beings in daily life, the lack of immediacy in contacts, and the resultant loneliness we frequently witness today have their roots in man's alienation from his own personal human center."[1]

It has been my professional experience that loss of self encompasses matters of quality of living, accomplishments or the lack of them, and meeting or falling short of one's ideals as well as success in relationships. Failure at these is as relevant and crucial in fostering hopelessness as the knowledge of one's inevitable demise. I hold with Kierkegaard that we are always well aware of the loss of a limb, a wife, or a $5 bill. However, the loss of self in its many subtle manifestations is not well-understood. The self sometimes slips away; only the fortunate get a warning signal. Atrophy from disuse, whether of one's limb or of one's liberty, is a particularly painful deprivation since it is a largely self-inflicted condition. It is bad enough that fate, biology, and the ravages of time diminish one, but to allow parts of the self to slip away passively is particularly distressing.

The deprivation often is part of the renunciation that is expected of a wife, even if she had an autonomous life before marriage. In an interview with Arthur Bell, Rhonda Fleming describes what happened to her when she got married.[2]

"I married Hall Bartlett for love and security. He wanted me to quit my career and I was ready to go along with it. I sold my home. I quit acting. I became completely dependent on a man for the first time in my life. Till then I was self-supporting, my career always came first, and I had never been solely dependent on anyone. And till then no one had said the magic words, 'quit working,' in that sweet sweet way."

Gradually she stopped seeing her friends. She began to live his life. "I was not aware of any resentment, but I began to see what happened to me. I relied on him for every dollar. Sometimes I had to beg for money. We went to Brazil where he was producing *The Sandpit Generals* and I did the dirty work, the typing, the office routine. I put on weight and lost my vivaciousness. I was becoming a dullard, not the woman I was before. I lost my backbone. All my roots were gone and I was frightened." Her dependence on her husband was painful and humiliating. In time she got a divorce and resumed her own career.

The loneliness wrought by the separation from one's imaginative and creative processes characterizes corporate life. The exigencies of corporate conformity require the renunciation of those simple pleasures that come from being a little wild, a bit eccentric—from doing one's own thing. The pressure of having to appear mature, cooperative, and conservative necessitates abandonment of playfulness and far-out behavior. For husband *or* wife to indulge in any of these might jeopardize his status and job. They are given up dutifully—and painfully. Ideally new pleasures might replace the old, new gratifications might be substituted for now inappropriate ones. But there is no guarantee that this

97

does or can happen. As so many older people sadly reflect, nature seems to frown on both regeneration and innovation.

Corporate executives may be paying heavily in little-suspected ways for the loneliness that their worklife style imposes on them. Chapters 2 and 5 pointed out some effects of the stresses generated by uprooting. Less specific but just as dangerous in the long run is their addiction for instance to tobacco and alcohol, which is quietly exacting a far higher toll in illness and death than is sensationalized heroin in all the ghettos of America. Also the suicide rate of middle-aged men is greater than that of women, and more management men go mad than are ever reported because of protective agencies. Having to live lives of rootlessness without strong community ties, having to produce and succeed often at the expense of wives and children, having to work in an atmosphere of chronic distrust and suspiciousness of both competitors and their own team have had brutalizing effects on character and ego.

After years of adherence to *machismo* behavior without truly belonging to a family or supportive community, it is little wonder if later in life the alert and cunning executive develops into a pathetic, paranoid personality. What has happened in essence is that his loneliness, partly chosen perhaps but partly forced on him as a condition of his success, has overwhelmed him. Quixotically, if such a man seeks psychiatric help, he frequently presents the complaint that he has been betrayed by—of all people—his wife. And typically, as in the following example, the wife's paramour is named as a good friend and superior at work.[3]

In the case of this patient, the circumstances of his life had changed, and the fragile equilibrium by which he lived was seriously disturbed— disturbed by events a person would ordinarily be expected to deal with. His children were now grown, contemplating marriage. Younger people were coming up in the business, and his position was becoming insecure. He was getting short of breath and had a dizzy spell now and then; his friends were dying of heart disease; his prowess, mental, physical, and sexual, was waning.

His mental health had shown signs of strain at various points in his life, but nothing had led him to seek help. As a child he had suffered night terrors and bedwetting. At puberty he had become panicky at the sight of his newly growing pubic hair. In his late adolescence he had had the feeling that he might have cancer of the throat. During his college years there had been a period of several months of worry that his studying might lead to blindness. Several more brief periods of nervousness during his marriage had occurred. He was usually aloof and restrained in his relations with his wife, but he sentimentalized about his children; he had cried at their birthdays and graduations—his babies were growing up.

He looked back on his childhood as completely happy, and therefore no inquiry was "needed" in this area. His parents had been good to him; he had had only feelings of love for his younger sister. As far as he was concerned, his chief misery had started a year earlier, with his "heartbreak" about his wife and his purported best friend. There never had been and there was not now anything wrong with his mind. Of course he was now nervous and couldn't sleep at night. But who wouldn't be nervous to the point of contemplating suicide if confronted by the agony of such a conspiracy?

Perhaps this man's difficulty was that he had lived long enough for his destiny to catch up with him. If he had died five years earlier, he would have concluded his life a successful individual, with the praise and love of those around him. His name would have been untarnished. Now he had run out of fuel, and he was a pitied creature, bringing humiliation to himself, his wife, and his children, who were both victims and witnesses of his fall.

Although he was brought down by the rigors of middle age, the roots of his difficulties lay in his earliest formative years. The agonies of child-hood, with grave hostilities against and alienation from his parents and his sister, were buried under conventional, acceptable sentiments. He loved happy thoughts and covered his memories with happy, gaily col-ored wrapping paper. We can only speculate what fantasies of betrayal, infidelity, abandonment, and humiliation he had suffered in that "most happy" home of his childhood. Perhaps it is unfair to do this type of retrospective construction for verification of theory, as psychiatrists do. But it would be naive to believe that a person's troubles were born today. As Santayana said, those who cannot remember the past are con-demned to repeat it.

Now, back to the question of why he should want to create a world of torment to live in, one in which he was cuckolded and rejected in-stead of one in which he was loved and respected. Without going into the technicalities, suffice it to say that in the overall picture, he gained relief from lifelong, pent-up, tormenting hostility and rage by creating a deus ex machina that cleansed him to pure innocence—the complete perfidy of those who purported to love him. In his role as victim of his wife and best friend, he established that the unholy alliance of woman and man now ruined his life as had another union of woman and man in the past. With such an alignment of tyranny against him, how could he reasonably be expected to function with the dignity and grace of a man of responsibility?

The sense of declining power in his business life added to his isolation. He felt he was losing the respect of others and was being reduced to an inanimate object—deadwood. Few people are lonelier than the man who fails in his work. If he does not succumb to some psychosomatic illness, he may become paranoid, alcoholic, or suicidal. Without success or achievement, the stress of his competitive existence inevitably overwhelms him.

In the real world the patient's importance was lessening. But how was he important in his created world of perfidy? Strangely enough he had a feeling of personal exaltation that of all the women available, the boss had chosen his wife for his paramour. The president of a large corporation, apparently happily married, a pillar in the community, was risking everything to carry on an affair with his wife! Even if she was a scoundrel, he now had proof that his wife, despite her age and plainness, was a choice woman whom a man of importance would run after at great risk. Although in fancied defeat he had the satisfaction of feeling that he had lost a prize to the best of competitors.

Cases like this one are far from rare in clinical practice. Often as not the husband maintains his delusion of his wife's infidelity in spite of massive evidence to the contrary. He has hired detectives; their reports are negative. He has examined her underclothes for telling spots; there have never been any. If he makes his obsessive suspicions known, her protestations of innocence and the pleas of friends, relatives, and children avail nothing. Just so did Shakespeare's King Leontes convince himself that his wife had betrayed him with his old friend Polixenes on the single ground that Polixenes had agreed to extend his visit when invited to do so by the queen.

The loneliness that corporate wives universally complain of covers a panoply of feelings, fears, and frustrations that they have neither the rhetoric nor the courage to articulate. "Loneliness" becomes the acceptable word, meaning something entirely different for each woman: "Being away from my familiar surroundings has made me lonely." "My husband's being away so much leaves me lonely." "It's lonely when my children go off to school." "I have no one to talk to, no one to cook for, no one to go to a movie with." "I'm frightened at night."

Left without human companionship, a person feels abandoned, a particular form of deprivation that taxes any human being. Yet there is more to this feeling than what results from the departure or absence of the other. In considering adult women who suffer "loneliness," it will not do to label them "children" or "spoiled" or "hysterical."

It is disconcerting to read in *Today's Health* that the Dartnell Corp. learned, apparently from "experts," that the distress wives suffer is due

100

to their emotional immaturity.[4] So, we are told, when a woman feels trapped with her home, children, and husband, and "when sitters become a problem, it is easy for boredom, loneliness and worry to overtake her." In other words the woman's discontent is of her own doing; she had better overcome her childishness for the good of husband and corporation. Instead of being of help to her psychologically, such a message has the effect of increasing her self-doubt and self-hate when the very opposite is desperately needed by this often perplexed and overwhelmed person.

After diagnosing the lonely woman as being emotionally immature, the article catalogs some "practical" measures in case she is also a worrier: buy a dog for protection, install an extra lock system, and buy electric garage doors. All these plus other devices to allay the fears of apprehensive wives suggest that the dangers lurk from without. It would appear that rather than lessening anxiety, these measures have the effect of increasing it. Such devices can only add credence to irrational fears and fantasies.

The real dangers that women feel are far more complex than can be represented by an intruder. Calling a woman names, psychiatric or other, and locking her in a fortress against purported external dangers may succeed in increasing her self-doubts to the point where she may worry about her sanity. Such "helpfulness" attacks all but the real problems, as is illustrated by the following case.[5]

A 26-year-old married woman, a teacher by profession, was referred from an adjoining community by her family doctor for an emergency consultation. She came with her husband, who, in his desire to be completely helpful, wished to sit in on the interview and was chagrined when I told him that this did not seem necessary. The patient was an attractive young woman whose features were distorted by an expression of abject fear. She had a wide-eyed stare that had led physicians to think she might be suffering from a glandular disorder. But thorough examinations proved to be negative.

She stated that in the past six months she had become anxious and depressed and was apprehensive that she was losing her mind and would be committed to the large mental hospital in the vicinity. She reported no current problems other than possibly the possessive demands of her mother. These upset her at times, but they were nothing new. She was well-satisfied with her marriage of five years and described her husband as loving, devoted, and now utterly distressed by her unhappiness. He would spare no amount of time and money to get her "over this thing." He had been married once before for a brief period and had suffered a great hurt from the failure of that union. He had extracted the promise

101

from the patient not to refer to that period in his life again, to let it be a completely closed book. This aroused the patient's curiosity, but she abided by her promise.

After this cursory explanation of the current situation, she immediately turned to the facts of her upbringing and early life, which she believed were the causes of her present difficulties. The younger of two children—her brother was three years her senior—she had been doted on because she had been born with a club foot. This had caused a great deal of consternation to the family, but successive operations had corrected the malformation almost completely; there was no noticeable residue. This had entailed financial hardship for the parents, but it had also meant that between the ages of 5 and 11, she had been hospitalized away from home for periods of up to six months. These separations had been very difficult for her, and until recent years when she had come to understand the beneficial results of her hospitalization, she had been bitterly hostile and antagonistic toward her mother for having left her alone in a strange environment. Her bitterness had changed to gratitude when she had realized that a cousin, now an adult, remained crippled with the same affliction because her parents had not been able "to part with her" so that she could undergo corrective surgery.

The patient described her father as a successful businessman who had had to retire in his 50s because he suffered episodes of severe depression and hypochondria. She recalled her mother as having been completely unsympathetic to his plight; she on the contrary had had strong positive feelings for her father. But her mother had had fears of her own, particularly of natural phenomena. Whenever there had been a thunderstorm or lightning at night, she had roused her two children from a sound sleep, taken them downstairs, and huddled with them in the basement of their home. Neither the patient nor her brother had had any such fears and at first were puzzled by this behavior. But in her late adolescence she had also become fearful of these things.

During subsequent interviews the patient told me more of her relationship with her mother—how she had written her every day from college, how she had acceded to her mother's wishes about dating, and yet how comfortable she had actually felt on being a considerable distance away from her. After her marriage, however, her husband had felt that they should live in the same community as her mother, which was also near the farm of his own parents. Here they had both entered into the social activities of the village and were quite popular.

His solicitude and attentiveness to her had earned him the reputation of being a model husband. He fully understood her problems with her mother, he told her, and would do everything he could to help her.

102

To get her somewhat out of her mother's orbit, he had built a home away from the village on a tract on his own parents' farm. To stay close by her so that he could allay her fears of the dark and of thunder and lightning, he had given up successive jobs that might keep him on the road overnight. He had had large floodlights installed around the house to discourage prowlers and had bought a police dog as further protection. On one occasion his company had promoted him to a job in a larger district in another state, but after some deliberation he had decided against it because it would take the patient away from her job, at which she was happy. His company had discharged him, but this had only increased his feelings of nobility. His religious feelings grew in intensity, in contrast with her own. He built an altar in their bedroom so they might pray together, confiding to her that his mainstay in living was prayer.

In this setting, instead of responding with well-being to her husband's solicitude, she had become increasingly depressed and fearful. Certain physical symptoms had appeared—pain around her heart and feelings of numbness in her arms and legs. Reassurances from her physician that there was nothing organically wrong made her more fearful since she now felt she couldn't even trust her own senses. Her physician treated her principally with sedatives and tranquilizers, which gave her momentary relief but actually lowered her confidence.

The entire relationship with the physician in fact proved to increase her fearfulness. In dealing with her he violated the principles of confidentiality that he would have adhered to in treating an ordinary physical disease, probably because he too was frightened by her condition. He reported on her to her husband and had many private conversations with him about her. The husband was allowed to call him frequently to find out whether this or that activity might be upsetting to her. All this of course made her doubt her own ability to get along.

The final blow, which reduced her to panic, was the regimen of tranquilizers her doctor put her on. Although she got some relief from the medication, the overall effect was to eliminate her last vestiges of confidence that she could properly evaluate and deal with things around her.

It was when her condition worsened on tranquilizers that she was sent for psychiatric help. The referring physician was very shaken by his experience with this patient and later in an informal communication indicated that he had at last realized he was an unwitting accomplice to her husband's machinations.

At this point it was only in the area of her job that she had confidence in her capabilities and judgment. She resisted the suggestions of her husband, friends, and physician that she take a leave of absence. They claimed that perhaps she was working too hard and that the children at school were making her nervous.

In the early months of her marriage, she had found pleasure in sexual relations with her husband. After they had moved to his family's homestead, these pleasurable feelings had left her, and sex had become fearful and revolting. It made her very ashamed to react this way to a husband who was so kind to her. Her husband had responded to her state by becoming even more solicitous and attentive. Now he would never leave her alone at home; he would forsake any business trip to be with her. When she had expressed her fear of losing her mind, he had suggested that she must confide in him, that married people should keep nothing from each other, reassuring her that no matter what she told him, he would understand. This had puzzled her further since she did not know what she could tell him or what he expected to hear.

These were the data the young woman gave in the initial interviews. We decided to begin psychotherapy. Two years of weekly sessions proved to be successful with her.

In the early hours of treatment, there was a barrage of questions from her and from her husband through her. Should she continue in her present job? Could she drive alone? Should her husband leave her alone overnight? Should she tell her mother she was seeing a psychiatrist? Should she see a doctor about her palpitations?

I handled each of these questions quite simply but firmly by taking the traditional neutral position of the therapist. I indicated to her that these were issues to be decided not by her mother, her therapist, or her husband but by herself. When she asked whether she could have a prescription for medication in case she suddenly became nervous or weak, I told her that if this happened, she would deal with it using her own resources, just as she had done during other stressful times—at her separation from home and the death of her father for example.

As was to be expected, the patient was at first distrustful of this type of treatment and interpreted it as indifference and unconcern. The loudest complaints, however, were from the husband, who declared he would not stand by and watch his wife suffer without medical relief. He would get to the bottom of this and would take her to the finest clinics in the country. But the patient herself resisted this, and the treatment was not interrupted. Appeals for emergency appointments when she felt panicky were denied. Likewise telephone calls for reassurance and for confirmation of appointments were discouraged.

In due course the patient came to grips with a most pertinent verity: that in her daily affairs only she had the necessary information to make decisions and act on them. All others—therapist, husband, mother, physician—acted in bad faith if they attempted to take over this function, even if she requested or demanded it of them.

This understanding led the patient to abandon her preoccupation with the past and to examine her present predicament. She saw that she was expected to play the helpless role far beyond actual need. Her feeling of gratitude toward her husband was replaced by a more realistic appraisal of the symbiosis they were involved in. And finally, she allowed herself to understand her husband's emotional difficulties and how they pertained to her. She could then see that he also had a fear of the dark and of being away from home and—most important of all—a need to be near his own parents. He was ashamed of these immaturities and projected them onto her. He hid his own need for parental protection by taking every opportunity to point up her helplessness, real or fancied. She was now angered by the fact that his principal words of endearment had been, "You're my little girl."

Now, without pills in her purse, she actively manages her own affairs. She remains at home alone *sans* hand holder. She no longer fears going insane or ending up in a mental hospital. A beneficial estrangement has taken place in the marriage, and roles and direction are being reappraised. The husband may enter therapy because of the new stresses placed on him by this realignment.

It is when the self is lost or communication with the self is severed that "the other" becomes so desperately important. Being alone then becomes a particularly fearful experience because there is literally no one at home. The *house* is empty because the *person* is. That is the tragic irony of the corporate wife's plight. She is scolded for being fearful and dependent; yet she is literally picked because she is dependent. Selflessness is deemed her most admirable attribute, but when she exhibits the inevitable effects of loss of self, she is called troublesome and lacking in emotional maturity.

The entire corporate life style encourages her to live solely through and by her husband; any personal aspiration or ambition is to be promptly extinguished. Any interest in or pleasure with other people is prohibited. And she is not to be fearful or lonely when he is away?

The mad rush to the suburbs has added to her miseries by cutting her off from the civic and cultural centers. The suburbs are like isolation wards, separated from all but the most superficial contact with fellow human beings and from the vitality of the city. Running away from the blacks and the poor, we have created suburban social starvation. We have actually taken pride in the distance we get from community and culture. To avoid being mugged we have accepted an isolation that probably produces more mind damage than could any mugger.

Not only does the corporate wife suffer this deprivation; it is foisted on children, who are located too far from public transportation to get to a library or museum, let alone a movie or playground. Any sense of independence is stifled by this lack of mobility. The enormous chauffeuring burden is placed on the wife, who later wonders why her children are so dependent. Separated from "live" human beings, real art, and civic activities, the mother and children turn to television, and gradually the substitute—the medium—comes to be thought better than real experiences. How audacious of the television announcer to say (as is required by law), "This program originates *live* from New York City."

In his perceptive book *The Pursuit of Loneliness,* psychologist Philip E. Slater writes:

> The emotional and intellectual poverty of the housewife's role is mainly expressed in the almost universal complaint "I get to talking baby talk with no one around all day but the children." . . . The idea of imprisoning each woman alone in a small, self-contained, and architecturally isolated dwelling is a modern invention dependent on an advanced technology. In Moslem societies, for example, the wife may be a prisoner but at least she is not in solitary confinement. In our society the housewife may move freely, but since she has nowhere to go and is not part of anything anyway her prison needs no walls.

Of the exodus from the city, Slater observes:

> But the flight to the suburb is in any case self-defeating, its goals subverted by the mass quality of the exodus. The suburban dweller seeks peace, privacy, nature, community and a child-rearing environment which is healthy and culturally optimal. Instead he finds neither the beauty and security of the countryside, the stimulation of the city, nor the stability and sense of community of the small town, and his children are exposed to a cultural deprivation equaling that of any slum child with a television set. Living in a narrow age-graded and class-segregated society, it is little wonder that suburban families have contributed so little to the national talent pool in proportion to their members, wealth, and other social advantages.

Moreover, as Slater points out, it is the wife who is ultimately left in the suburban trap because the man's work rescues him for most of the week, taking him to the city office, the plant, or on the road meeting real people and challenging problems.

> Consider the suburban living pattern: husbands go to the city and participate in the 20th century, while their wives are assigned the hopeless task of trying to act out a rather pathetic bucolic phantasy

THE ANATOMY OF LONELINESS

oriented toward the 19th. Men in their jobs must accept change—even welcome and foster it—however threatening and disruptive it may seem. . . . Such men tend to make of their wives an island of stability in a sea of change. The wife becomes a kind of memento, like the bit of earth that the immigrant brings from the old country and puts under his bed.[6]

William V. Shannon calls the suburban housewives "the new servant class," pointing out that with the family's second car, "They spend two to three hours every day as involuntary chauffeurs because there is no other way to get their children to music lessions, dental appointments, or friends' houses."[7] And this is but one aspect of the service role the suburban housewife is expected to play. The physical care and management of the ever-enlarging, status-proving home becomes her responsibility, and she can no longer find the inexpensive help of yesteryear. Her time is spent on things rather than people.

In sociologist Alice Rossi's study of young married college graduates, 65 percent of the women reported they conversed with their husbands less than two hours a day.[8] Similarly research shows that full-time homemakers spend an average of less than two hours a day in direct interaction with children. Women then devote to household chores four times as many hours as they do to interaction with husbands or children. Alice Rossi concludes that it is house care that keeps women at home more than child care. A great deception has been perpetrated against suburban women: while they might bow to their isolation because they think suburban living enhances communication with mate and children, they find that most of their day and energies are spent on menial, boring, and uncreative tasks—no different from the existence of serving maidens of the past.

Even modern technocratic gains have worked against women. It was the expectation for instance that modern appliances would so simplify domestic chores that a woman would be liberated from the household grind that was her grandmother's lot. Studies have shown that the very opposite is the case: the more automatic appliances in a home, the greater—not the fewer—the number of hours of regular household work. For although the amount of physical energy expended per task may be lessened, women have been brainwashed into standards of cleanliness that keep them chronically and inextricably bound. A home economist lamented to me that she met terrible resistance from women to whom she suggested that bed linen didn't have to be changed more often than once a week. One woman put fresh sheets on the beds daily; most changed them twice a week. Some candidly asked just what they were expected to do with the saved time!

107

It is not wide of the mark to say that such busy work attempts to fill the vacuum made by the absence of meaningful activity and the deprivations wrought of isolation and estrangement from human contact. And loneliness as well as stupefaction inevitably ensues when one is reduced to substituting routinized and contrived activities for the interpersonal and creative endeavors for which the mind was meant. Loneliness can be construed as the dread that results from the loss or diminution of parts of one's self that formerly gave pride and hope. Can these be derived from changing sheets every day?

It is this hierarchy of deprivations that makes the corporate wife appear so pathetically unresourceful. She is lonely, afraid of the night, and lost when her husband is away. To the resourceful and energized person, to be left alone is to be given the blessing of freedom. One becomes free of the onerous aspects of continuous togetherness. Rather than producing loneliness being alone might leave one free to pursue personal projects, unread books, and cooling friendships. But as existentialist Sartre remarked, probably having the unresourceful in mind, freedom is a curse.

Although transcultural study is beyond the scope and purpose of this book, we are beginning to hear more about the Japanese corporate wife now that that nation has become a major industrial power. Sister Mary Jacinta Shailer did her master's thesis in sociology studying company "widows" in Japan.[9] Their predicament is at least as bad as their American sisters'. The Japanese women too live on the fringes of Japan's large cities though not in individual homes as in America; their homes are in "large drab concrete housing complexes called *Danchi*." Sister Jacinta reports that these women, though well-educated, are expected to resign themselves to the chronic absence of their husband and to accept the care of their children as their sole occupation and gratification. Danchi husbands, commuters who work long hours, invariably ease their tensions with their favorite hostesses at bars and company parties. In contrast to the progress of husbands, the wives show "a dismaying picture of high-rise neuroses, alienation, loneliness, rising suicide, and mental decay."

The women lead housebound lives. They are reduced to spending their free time either watching television or in gossiping; apparently abandoning their own hopes for the future, they show "an almost obsessive concern for the future of their children, forcing most of them to attend heavy schedules of extra classes and music lessons."

The fierce competition that has arisen among these women over the accomplishments of their children has led to the coining of the derisive term—yes, you've guessed it—"Danchi mama." When these mothers feel they have promoted their children inadequately, their sense of failure leads to depression and suicide. Sister Jacinta reports a sharp increase in suicide among Japanese women. Underlying these tragedies is the fact that Japanese husbands do not like independence in their wives any more than do American executives. Despite financial benefits if the wife works, it causes them to lose face.

Thus when the Japanese husband says, "I never take my wife along," one shouldn't assume that all is dandy in Danchi.

One way of dispelling loneliness is to become a "kitchen sink" drinker. According to the National Council on Alcoholism, there are probably 5 million alcoholics in the United States today, with a ratio of 2 men for every woman. A decade ago the ratio was 5 to 1.[10] The reasons why women drink are reported to be boredom, depression, loneliness, marital problems, and children leaving home. Such problems are, at least partially, all related to a lack of personal autonomy.

Drinking in the suburbs is slightly easier than elsewhere, but the suburban housewife has to deal with certain problems, such as how to participate in car pools without causing accidents. One Connecticut woman reported, "I always take the early half of the afternoon car pool because I know I can't handle it later in the day."

Money helps mask the problem. "In a community like ours, it's easier to cover up," said Marie Fitzsimmons, director of the Alcoholism Guidance Center in Westport, Connecticut, a high-income community. "There's money for liquor, for psychiatry, for a housekeeper, all of which may work against coming to grips with the reality of alcoholism."

While the majority of corporate wives in our country continue to follow traditional patterns, increasing numbers are not only hearing but heeding the echoes of Women's Liberation or the promptings of their own independently discovered sense of loss of self. One such is featured in a *Life* magazine story of what it called a drop-out wife.[11] She is a 35-year-old college graduate, mother of three, wife of a "middle-level" business executive. With no great animosity or differences between her and her husband, without frequent separations, and with no money problems, Wanda Adams, finding her life increasingly "frustrating and suffocating," wanted out in her fourteenth year of marriage. There were no villains. It seemed a matter of personal growth. She is seeking this by going back to school and by working.

After her separation from her husband, she found herself "happier than I ever was": "In spite of the loneliness, the garbage of survival, and the occasional feeling of not wanting to be independent, I like myself better and I like other people better." Still on friendly terms with her husband, she neither asks for nor receives alimony. She lives with her daughter, the oldest child, in a commune arrangement with other women; the two boys are with their father.

Although she says that her life now is full of hassles, Ms. Adams finds solace in their being *her* hassles. She looks back at her married life as not rewarding or fulfilling. She was completely absorbed in her family role, with little outside life. "Our friends were always Don's business friends or friends of ours from college."

Her husband has acted as "mother and father" to the boys and has done remarkably well. We read the heading over pictures showing him doing household chores: "Unsuspected joys for a lone father." However, he enjoyed being married and contemplates marrying again. In the separation he has found that caring for his children (for the first time) has given him a sense of closeness he had never felt before. Parenthood after all is alien to most fathers. Many who allow themselves to fulfill the role reap enjoyable rewards.

What are we to make of this story? New sensationalism? The exception that again proves the rule? The story of the Adamses is and will be atypical of how corporate wives in general will behave. Perhaps it is unfortunate that more will not follow in the search.

But this story, like the movies of a few years ago, *Diary of a Mad Housewife* and *The Happy Ending,* are signs of the times. They are characterized by dissatisfaction with and alternatives to the conventional roles of married life rather than by tirades against the tyrannies of a husband. This is an era when wives are not railing against villains. On the contrary there is a growing recognition that both marital partners may be trapped by institutionalized expectations that are less than salutary for either, though the wife is more likely to start the rebellion (the greater sufferer understandably feeling more of the pressure). Wanda Adams must be endowed with a remarkable and much-to-be admired optimism to have dropped out of a pattern of living, 14 years and three children later, that most wives become reconciled to and endure silently.

Brought up and educated to know what one's "normal" role is, performing the duties of wife and mother for years, and obtaining the security and gratifications that accrue from the conventional life make the task of seeking independence no easy matter. That many fall on their face is easy to document.

While some studies find that divorced women are happier than married women, others show that anxiety and depression in divorced women is high. Conditioned from birth to think they should be married, many rush into a frantic search for another man to marry. Because they are actively trained to not want to be independent, it is a most difficult struggle for them to strive for autonomy, the natural birthright of self-respecting people. When they find Mr. Right, they hope he (unlike the previous, unsatisfactory husband) will truly communicate with them, that alienation will not be the order of the day this time.

Interestingly enough, though a dislike of independence is culturally inadmissible by a man, there are research findings that married men are happier than divorced men—perhaps showing that marriage, thought popularly to be the goal of every woman, is really an institution suited to and beloved by men.

The loneliness that comes with marriage is particularly severe because there is the expectation of the opposite. Since the Romantic period began, people have hoped that marriage would be a bastion against the disappointments of the world and the fears of self-doubt. Loneliness in marriage is particularly painful because one feels betrayed or abandoned, having had such great hopes. That these hopes were unrealistic and foredoomed to disappointment, that no human being can find in one other person all the passion, intellectual stimulation, warmth, and security that make life exciting as well as safe, makes it no less shattering when they fail.

A colleague, Thomas Szasz, sounds a caveat for those who would live through others: "A person cannot make another happy, but he can make him unhappy. This is the main reason why there is more unhappiness than happiness in the world."[12]

Being lonely when one is single is an acceptable idea; being lonely when one is actually eating, sleeping, and dwelling with another is indeed alarming. We can then understand the meaning of Chekhov's seeming contradiction: "If you are afraid of loneliness, don't marry."

PART III

Humans in Relations

SEXUAL MERGERS
AND SPIN-OFFS

A roll in the hay is good for you
But a man of gods has work to do.
ALAN DUGAN

THERE IS an amazing candor about the flagrantly double standard for American corporate sex. There has never been any attempt to hide the fact that corporate men expect sex as a natural reward for business success as well as a necessary implement for gaining that success. Not so with corporate wives. They undoubtedly have not been so chaste as the corporate image demands of them, but nonetheless they try to maintain an air of propriety.

Our largest American companies have admitted that female entertainers are often used to help land prospective customers—a necessary, probably tax-deducted business expense. Similarly conventions, national meetings, and the required business trips are conducive to errant sex for the husband. At such places the ordinary restraints of home and community are absent; he has the freedom of anonymity, which is often enough to overcome the inhibiting code of fidelity and familial responsibility. Many men feel that they deserve a good time as a reward for hard work and extraordinary effort. And there are women who similarly feel less restrained at conventions and will cooperate in sexual adventures.

A major British overseas airline offered the opportunity of dates in England for men who would travel with it. This promotion venture, officially discontinued at present, was directed toward the American market. Pressure from Parliament caused the airline to stop the campaign, though it wouldn't be surprising if unofficial accommodations were still available. In domestic air travel one Texas-based carrier makes no secret of its belief that its burgeoning business has resulted not from its excellent safety record but from its policy of having its stewardesses flirt with male passengers. It is known as and likes to be called "the love airline." The sexual pitch in air-travel advertising seems to be emerging as a most fruitful one. The airline that reduced fares for wives with the suggestion "Take her along" or "Give her Hawaii for Christmas" had limited success. These slogans have had far less pull than the sexually unsubtle "I'm Karen, fly me to Miami" (across state lines?).

An article titled "Rent-a-Girl Enterprises Flourishing Across U.S." presented the world's oldest profession in modern corporate terms: "In an era in which the women's liberation movement is reminding the public that a woman is a person and not just an entertainment diversion, female escort services are blossoming in certain areas of the country."[1] The services available range from straight-out prostitution to the polished look-but-don't-touch companionship offered by a concern called Rent-a-Bird. One reason for the success of this industry is that "The stepped-up mobility of modern life, stimulated by the airplane, has created a rapidly growing group of executives who find themselves away from home to attend conventions or work in their company's branch office for brief periods of time and, as a result, the demand for leisure-time company has increased." It could be anticipated that the needs of executives with money would stimulate the ingenuity of entrepreneurs.

Society thus typically tries to remedy the disease of loneliness for the so-called stronger sex—but not for the weaker. No such provision is made for lonely corporate wives back at the split-level ranch. And if there were an agency called Rent-a-Wolf, small children as well as neighbors and a host of other observers would have a lot to say about such a figure appearing at the front door at 7:30 P.M.—and more to say about the mother-wife who welcomed him in.

The cure for loneliness that prosperous American men are chasing may be less sexual than it appears at first glance. Take for example the Playboy Club phenomenon. *Playboy* magazine itself is clearly an example of antiseptic sex—both the pictures and the articles are much more mechanical than sensual. The clubs themselves enforce the look-but-don't-touch ethic. In a *New York Times Magazine* article J. Anthony Lukas quotes a spokesman:

> Our statistics show that the average Playboy keyholder is 10 years older than the average Playboy reader. They're in their late 30's or early 40's, the Allis-Chalmers manager or the Colgate salesman in on a business trip. Look at them. They're not in here after girls. They're quite happy to have a meal and a brew and ogle the bunnies a bit.
>
> So what would happen if you brought all those swingers in here? These guys would have to start wondering: Could I really pick up

that girl and, if I could, and if I actually got her home, could I perform in bed? It's a threat they don't want and I don't think we're ever going to give it to them.

Lukas comments: "Hefner has been credited with an important insight in anticipating, assisting or actually initiating the American 'sexual revolution.' But perhaps his insight was of a different kind altogether—recognizing the profound sexual anxiety in many American men and realizing that the road to success lay in indulging that anxiety, not exacerbating it."[2]

Perhaps the life experience of the American male has made him unable to enjoy sex and sensuality as much as he could were he not so competitive—in the bedroom as well as in the office. Rollo May, the psychotherapist, writes: "*Playboy* . . . gets its dynamic from a repressed anxiety in American men that underlies even the fear of involvement. This is the repressed anxiety about impotence. Everything in the magazine is beautifully concocted to bolster the illusion of potency without ever putting it to the test or challenge."[3]

Of course that psychotherapists even equate performing in bed with a "test or challenge" shows that our culture considers sex far from a pleasure.

The opening of a new Playboy resort hotel in New Jersey that Lukas covered could be described as many things—but clearly "sexy" would not be one of them:

> Middle-aged couples, the women in floor-length evening gowns, fox-trotted around the floor. Hefner, at a front table, nodded his head to the heavy fifties beat. Mike Murphy, a Playboy publicity man, suggested we drop down to a party at the indoor pool. When we arrived a half-dozen bunnies in pastel suits were paddling about in the heated Jacuzzi, giggling almost shyly at the male guests who stared uncomfortably back from poolside. . . . The next evening thousands of New Jerseyans poured into the hotel. . . . They came in families—housewives with blond beehives piled on their heads, grandmothers in print dresses, swarms of snowsuited children—scarcely noticing the occasional flustered bunny trying to fight her way through the jammed hallways.[4]

Is the Playboy Club our version of the Japanese geisha house? John M. Lee writes that American businessmen traveling or working in Japan are growing "wary" and "weary" of the geisha party, which has become the routine (and high-priced) entertainment for foreign customers.[5] Contrary to the fantasies of most Americans, it "is as erotic as a church supper." Contact with the geisha girls is limited to a few pats and

117

squeezes. However, further arrangements can be made if desired. "Of course, I never take my wife along," a Japanese executive explained, "even if he [the visitor] brings his wife. The American wives seem to come on the third or fourth trip." Such togetherness is an American habit, what with entire families visiting the Playboy resort hotels.

Whether her husband roams to Japan or across town, however, the American corporate wife seems resigned to accepting his sexual dalliances if they are done discreetly (not bragged about). Lois Wyse reports that only 2 percent of the wives in her survey considered a husband's unfaithfulness a reason for having affairs of their own. Apparently even they consider sexual adventurousness one of the successful man's prerogatives. In addition, according to Ms. Wyse, 75 percent of the women "never have considered an affair."[6]

Ms. Wyse's subjects though are "Mrs. Successes," as the title of her book shows. Their viewpoints probably contrast sharply with the attitudes and behavior of women in the lower economic brackets. Among low-income people, I have noted that wives fiercely resent their husbands' spending money on other women because there is trouble making ends meet at home. It is the economic dimension rather than the sexual one that stimulates their ire. Some would even welcome being relieved of sexual demands were it not for having to skimp and save and wear shoddy clothes while the family income is spent on drinks and motel rooms.

For the wives of wealthy men of course this is not a problem. Yet economic imperatives may be at work here too, as Chapter 6 pointed out. It may be that rich men's wives say they are not interested in affairs because they are reluctant to risk the loss of financial power for themselves and their children. As unhappy as the couple may be, the husband's losing his job or status is potentially disastrous for both. One can readily confirm Lois Wyse's finding that wives of rich men are loyal. She writes: "Ask a question about the state of a rich woman's marriage, and you will find that *her* marriage is excellent; *her* marriage is happy, but Mary-at-the-Club really has marital problems."[7] Since everything is relative, how convenient that there always is a Mary-at-the-Club who is either ingenuous or honest about her marital existence, especially after a few drinks. She is a convenience in that by comparison other marriages appear harmonious and tolerable.

While a cuckolded executive loses credibility and prestige in the business world, a man's sexual activity—again if done with discretion—may actually enhance his image of power (potency) in accordance with *machismo* expectations. A sexually chaste male, married or not, is under suspicion of lacking in virility and adventuresomeness. For these reasons as well as the financial prospects, corporate wives are not mortally alienated by the sexual inconstancies of their partners, as their poorer sisters may be, and on the main seek no revenge or retaliation as long as husbands return to the fold.

Occasionally and exceptionally a spirit of sexual rebelliousness and self-assertiveness does surface in an otherwise conventional woman. And when it does the results are apt to be volcanic. One such instance scandalized the community and nearly cost a corporate wife her head, emotionally speaking. As we will see, when she did rebel she left little room for retreat or rehabilitation.[8]

A 40-year-old woman, mother of two adolescent boys, returned to her profession of teaching after her motherly chores at home seemed completed. Following a refresher course she applied for a job and was accepted in a nearby school system. She was delighted to return to her work after a lapse of 15 years though she noted that things had changed a great deal and there was much catching up to do. Always a hard and enthusiastic worker, she welcomed the new challenge. Yet it wasn't easy. Although she was youthful in appearance and spirit, most of the school's personnel were much younger. They were generally kind, but older people were under the suspicion of being rigid, old-fashioned in methods, and unable to take or properly understand student problems and antics.

In the course of her work, she was befriended by a 24-year-old teacher, a recent graduate of a teachers college. They would meet in the dining room and chat about school problems. He seemed to prefer her company to that of people his own age. She gave him no overt encouragement but was nonetheless very pleased to have a friend who was both patient and generous in helping her with school problems that otherwise seemed overwhelming.

In general their friendship was fairly well tolerated by others, both faculty and students. Her husband, a successful businessman in his 50s, kidded her at times about her "young lover." He had not approved of her going back to teaching but had indulged her, feeling that in three months or so she would wear herself out and return to the fold.

This did not happen. Instead her interest in her home life diminished as she became increasingly enthralled with her work. At the same time her friendship with the young teacher ripened into a romance, and they professed love for each other. She experienced a sexual excitement and gratification with him that had been absent from her marriage for at least 10 years.

One day she informed her husband that she could no longer "live a lie" and that she and the young man wanted to marry. The husband at first ridiculed such a proposition and such a match; to him she had

119

gone crazy—probably one of those change-of-life insanities. He was not going to cooperate in any divorce proceedings that would make him the laughingstock of the community. Rather than taking part in any further "irrational" discussion, he demanded that she consult a psychiatrist, one whom they both knew socially. If the psychiatrist thought they should be divorced, the husband said he would agree.

She was interviewed by the psychiatrist, who was visibly dismayed by the turn of events with his friends, she later related. He advised her to undergo psychotherapy before she made any drastic change in her life. She was reluctant to do this but finally agreed since it made some sense to resist acting precipitately. Therapy was begun. In the course of eight months he "found" and imparted to her the infantile derivatives of her present behavior. She was told that she could not accept growing old, that she was narcissistic, and that she had alas been taken in by Women's Liberation rhetoric. She was reminded that she would bring disgrace to her prominent husband and adolescent boys. Their egos might be shattered by her "acting out." And finally, the therapist found that her attraction to the young man was a displacement of a pathological attraction toward her sons.

She listened to these interpretations and tried to suggest other motives, such as love and the need for a second chance. The therapist discounted these as rationalizations and resistance. Therapy made no dent either in her attitude or behavior; she continued in her romance with her young lover. The therapist then recommended tranquilizers as a necessary adjunct to therapy. She agreed to try them because she felt herself becoming increasingly nervous. She was now plagued by sleeplessness and agitation, which to the therapist confirmed his original diagnosis of "nervous breakdown" with the "sexual misbehavior" as a principal symptom.

But the therapy did not seem to improve the condition; one night she was found in a semicomatose state as a result of an overdose of tranquilizers and sleeping capsules. At this point she was hospitalized in a psychiatric ward, and the diagnosis of her "mental aberration" was again substantiated.

Through the intervention of her brother, an attorney, she gained her release from the hospital. After a stormy course and now with the moral support of her brother and her parents, she won her divorce and left the community. She and her friend traveled to another part of the country and were married. Her adolescent sons chose to remain with their affluent father.

In all, her love had a multiplicity of motives, some good, some bad—but hers. Who is to say that she was either "sick" or "healthy"? Is it not enough to say that she was merely a human being with a full set of strivings and longings that she, unlike most other people, had the courage to reveal and act on? There is little doubt that she was nearly done in—not by any internal sickness but by the pressures of external forces, including psychiatry, that demanded renunciations from her in the name of mental health. Ultimately she did not recant—a Joan of Arc in her own way.

Marital life in corporate America is beset by all sorts of ills. John Barnett writes that the jet age adds to the misery because it increases the time an executive spends away from home.[9] The divorce rate of corporate couples is not high, but this, Barnett feels, reflects the necessity to continue "arrangements" to give the appearance of stability. Marriages are preserved in name only by "weary, indifferent men and women" because corporations are apt to look with suspicion on men who can't control their own households and whose marital problems go public. It is typical for wives to cooperate with even tyrannical husbands to hide these difficulties whenever possible.

As people stay together for the corporation, they do so also "for the children." The specter of what supposedly happens to children of broken homes is enough to keep many marriages together. It is true that children want to preserve errant behavior as their very own monopoly; they almost universally do not like divorce. But it is highly doubtful that they suffer the dire effects often described. On the contrary the dishonesty and hypocrisy involved in the staying-together-for-the-children situation may disillusion the supposed beneficiaries and at the same time place an intolerable burden of guilt on their shoulders.

The toll that the dead and empty marriage takes in human misery is incalculable. The marriage is preserved at the expense of the parties involved. This social tragedy imitates the medical irony—the operation was a great success, but the patient died. John Barnett catalogs many emotional ills: chronic loneliness, alcoholism, and excessive dependence on children. As we learn more about the epidemiology of our serious physical illnesses, such as heart diseases, strokes, diabetes, asthma, high blood pressure, and the other scourges of middle age, their connection with social tension is becoming increasingly evident. One can state almost categorically that the dead marriage contributes just as significantly to the development of these disorders. What greater frustration can there be than the feeling of being inextricably bound to your main source of misery, your mate?

Sexual incompatibility is the reason given for much of the hostility and misunderstanding in marriage. Often the sexual needs of one do not mesh with those of the other. Of course it is never as simple as that. So much of the rest of living seeps into the conjugal bed, cooling it to a point of discomfort and dissatisfaction.

Obviously young men, perhaps unconsciously, choose wives who are more likely to facilitate than to obstruct their careers. William H. Whyte, Jr., found in 1951 that young men frequently outmarry themselves, that is, pick women who are superior to themselves in social and financial status.[10] These men have a great advantage *if* they are able to hold up their own end. If on the other hand they lack the ability or cunning to climb the ladder surely and swiftly, there is trouble. The trainer is better than the fighter, who must ultimately enter the ring alone. If he falters and slides, the trainer may turn away in disgust—or even throw in the towel.

A man who marries a woman brighter than himself has this problem. If he fails the woman may become contemptuous of him, feeling that she has wasted her time and effort. She is apt to bemoan her fate in having attached her destiny to such an ill-fated, burned-out star. If she remains married to him—and frequently she must, for viable options are meager or absent—she diminishes what is left of him by never failing to show her disappointment either directly or in a thousand subtle but no less devastating ways. She will then turn her back on him, sexually and otherwise, and spend her energies on her growing sons as young hopefuls in the struggle for success. This, as one might surmise, places a double burden on the children: to try to fulfill their mother's burning ambitions and to maintain some kind of human relationship with the discredited and humiliated father.

If the man who outmarries himself does rise in his career, he will ultimately eclipse his wife in mental development and stature. Confronted by complex problems and challenges, traveling a great deal, meeting new people, and exchanging ideas at meetings and conferences, they are expanding their minds constantly. On the other hand the wife rarely can share directly in these exciting and broadening activities. Caring for the household and raising children, as important as these endeavors are, cannot provide the mental stimulation that living in the outer world does. Although no husband will verbalize it, he senses the intellectual gap. He says the opposite: how bright she is, how she is the brains of the family, how he hasn't read a book in 10 years but she is an avid reader. Yet he knows that he cannot discuss anything but domestic issues with her. And characteristically at this point he tells her heartily that she is a wonderful "mother" without whom the household would fall apart. At some stage she may detect how patronizing a term that is—what a pat on the head. When he calls her "Mother," the moment of truth has clearly arrived.

122

The man who undermarries often feels that the woman will be grateful for the material gains and the new status that his achievement will give her and will thus not become overly demanding. She will love and take good care of a fine house the likes of which she has never known before, and she will most likely be cooperative and not question his absences or dalliances. She will be preoccupied with domestic chores and fill up her life with many children.

However, difficulty often arises when the young man has a meteoric rise. The wife, unschooled in such matters as elegant entertainment, has great difficulty grooming herself in the thousand and one social graces that are expected of her at certain levels of society. Domestic help may be brought in, but this rarely suffices to allay the wife's self-doubt. She often experiences a dread of social events. At this point she may develop psychosomatic symptoms that keep her from attending certain functions. She may become light-headed for example at large gatherings of people. As a further defense she may be overtaken by phobic reactions that prevent her from flying in a plane or even riding in an elevator.

Such a person becomes reluctant to invite people over, fearful that her social ineptness will show. She then needs alcohol or tranquilizers or both to get her though the evening. She was happier when life was simpler. While she is grateful for her new advantages and luxuries, the people in the new world she has been catapulted into behave and speak differently from anyone she has known. Instant education is impossible. Her husband is now visibly irritated but usually too protective to reveal openly that his purported asset is now a liability. The simple, obedient wife who seemed to be such an advantage earlier is now a source of embarrassment for him. Why hasn't she grown with him? He didn't go to college either, but he can always manage to converse with the best of them. She will by contrast shrink away, excusing herself to look after the dinner or the children or her headache.

This sad story is by no means the exclusive preserve of corporate America. Political life, with similar meteoric advances of husbands, finds childhood-sweetheart wives ill-equipped for the new role that has been thrust on them. Doctors' and lawyers' wives, who have often put their husbands through school at the expense of their own educations, frequently are shelved in their middle years for younger, more educated replacements.

Unequal growth and experience, which is the fate of so many couples in corporate America, often makes for an eventual sexual distancing as it erodes other areas of living. A husband's travels broaden him sexually as well as intellectually. He is exposed to many new adventures that may make him discontented with previous modes of behavior. This

123

is less likely to happen to the stay-at-home, chaperoned wife, and she consequently retains her traditional, decorous beliefs and attitudes. She may be shocked and horrified by new sexual ways that a husband may try to introduce into their marriage.

Tom and Ethel grew up in the same neighborhood in a Midwestern rural community. They were brought up in a fundamentalist religious tradition. High school sweethearts, they exchanged vows of eternal devotion to each other. He went on to college; she worked as a secretary and saved money toward their marriage, which occurred on the day of his graduation. They were both virgins at the time of their marriage as far as they knew or cared, and their sexual adjustment was fine.

Tom got a job with a farm machinery corporation and was well-liked and trusted by employers as well as customers. In due time they moved to the city of the home office. Their married life appeared ideal. They had three children in seven years; she was known as a wonderful wife, mother, and housekeeper.

Then the inevitable traveling began for Tom. He was beset by loneliness. At first he resisted the temptations of opportunities for extramarital sex because of his devotion to his wife and family and because of his strong religious beliefs. But he finally succumbed to the pressures of the world and had a series of liaisons, which he kept secret. In the course of these, he was introduced to oral-genital sex, which he had heard of and read about but had never experienced or suggested to Ethel. He enjoyed this new sexual practice and looked forward to it on his trips.

Although able to perform and enjoy sex in the conventional way, this Bible-belt Portnoy found fellatio and cunnilingus ecstatic experiences. He had some moral qualms about these activities at first, but they were easily dispelled by conversations with colleagues who freely admitted to similar practices. The frequent allusions to it in modern literature reassured him that he had not invented the idea. He then wondered why he had been denied this pleasure for so long.

As if to share altruistically a new-found toy, he gingerly approached Ethel to practice oral sex with him. He expected some resistance, but he never anticipated the disaster that ensued. She was thrown into a state of shock. Her husband, she was certain, had an alliance with Satan himself. Such practices, she knew, were not just sinful but perverted as well. She would have none of them or of him. In her mind sex could only be done in the "normal" manner; she would never veer from the missionary position—the husband on top and the woman in her proper place: underneath. Not only would she not participate in the abominations he was suggesting, but she could never again trust anyone who had indulged in them. At one stroke almost complete disillusionment set in. After that she resisted any form of sexual contact with him.

Hurt and dismayed, Tom recoiled and returned to conjugation as usual with Ethel when she would allow him to approach her. He did try from time to time to make his wife engage in the new practices, but predictably she resisted. She became increasingly enraged and consulted her minister, who also did not condone such behavior.

With Tom's persistence and Ethel's indignation both escalating, the marriage ended in divorce. Ethel returned with her children to the family homestead in the Midwest. The irony of this story is that Ethel later remarried, and with her second husband she led an active sex life that included oral-genital activity, which she found both acceptable and exciting with him.

Tom, in introducing his new game to Ethel, acted perhaps out of love and devotion. Yes, you might call him ingenuous and naive. Most men who become sexually more sophisticated than their house-ridden wives know when to leave well enough alone. They dichotomize their sexual life between home and garden. They perform their tricks on the outside and behave routinely and conventionally in the marital bed. In this way suspicions are not aroused and misunderstandings are avoided.

Sexuality is at best a delicate and fragile flower. It suffers a natural attrition and diminution in the normal course of marriage. Although 15 or 20 years of marriage may heighten feelings of dependence and mutuality in a hundred different ways, time has a dampening effect on excitement, passion, and fun. How ironic that the most pleasurable sexual experiences people have are often with perfect strangers and not with those they love. Perhaps sex is an unreal state that suffers irreparably from day-to-day realities.

A recent study by a group of cardiologists showed that *marital* sex was safe for cardiac patients because it barely raised the pulse and blood pressure. *Illicit* sex, however, could prove fatal for them, as can be confirmed by motel managers. Some would call this divine retribution, but more likely the cause is the heightened excitement of being involved with a stranger.

When the sexual thrill fades in marriage, people unfortunately blame either the partner or themselves for ineptness, indifference, lack of love, or sickness. They fail to accept the existential deterioration worked by prolonged familiarity. They forget that there are no passionate love poems written about marriage partners.

The inroads of familiarity by no means affect husbands alone of course. John Barnett describes the paradox of a wife's suffering sexual deprivation because of her husband's traveling and then refusing to have relations with him on his return. Whether out of pique or hidden sexual politics as described by Kate Millett, she becomes negative about intimacy even when the circumstances appear salutary.

The don't-touch-me syndrome has probably existed as long as civilization itself. What woman in her sexual lifetime has not spoken those words? Ultimately they are an expression of a basic human right. Most often they are said in anger and disappointment: touching is affirmation, withholding is denial. At times a woman exhibits revulsion for her husband's touch when the reasons are repressed and unknown.

Couples otherwise seemingly loving and compatible find themselves faced with the dilemma of one mate's cringing at the touch of the other. Instead of pleasure, sexual relations now bring distaste to the point of nausea for one and complete bewilderment for the other. As one might suspect there is far more than sex alone involved.

Such was the case with a young corporate wife who sought therapy because of her perplexing untoward sexual reactions. She loved her husband, a rising young engineer. She had made three moves in six years with him, tolerated his almost weekly absences, and took care of the household and the children. But one night and thereafter, she would not allow him to touch her. They had been married for six years without incident. The trouble seemed to begin about three months after the birth of their second daughter.

Her husband was a well-educated man of 33, socially as well as professionally skilled, who was continent in his habits and gave no indication of infidelity or discontent. He was a self-made man, having worked his way through college, and he supported his family in a comfortable style. In his attitude toward his wife, he was generally supportive but never intrusive or demanding. His general behavior made their problem all the more perplexing. If he had been a martinet or a cunning Odysseus, then one could readily point the accusing finger, but this was not the case.

She was unlike him in character makeup. Although also well-educated, she described herself as a timid person, never at ease in a group, lacking confidence in her ability to manage her own and family affairs. She looked to her husband for advice and instruction in many of the decisions about the household. She conceded that she was generally good with the children, but she worried about doing them psychic harm. Yet she gladly spent her whole day caring for them and never felt either bored or deprived in this activity. She was most comfortable in her role as mother, never finding her children's touch or demands anything but welcome and desirable.

She felt less comfortable with her husband in the evenings, for she could contribute little to worldly conversation and was in awe of his erudition and poise. In company she generally deferred to him. She depreciated her own education and skills, describing herself as the plodder who did the work. She had gotten good grades but said she never really learned anything; she felt she should not be expected to be informed on any subject.

During treatment her one positive attitude was her disdain for her mother, whom she blamed for ruining her life. She had been told by a psychologist that her mother was "sick" and that it was a miracle she had grown up as well as she did. She had been an only child, the recipient of all her mother's love and also the target for all her wrath.

As analysis continued she began to reveal both facts and fantasies about her parents' marital life. She said that her mother had harassed her father, and she wondered how he could take the nagging and depreciation. In growing up she had experienced continual embarrassment at being a witness to this seemingly unfair struggle. Although without any concrete knowledge about it, she fantasied that her parents had never had sexual relations after her birth—that her mother had withheld sex from her father as part of her punitive regimen.

The mother had turned to her daughter for solace for the frustrations she had felt so acutely in her marriage (one of the many unfortunate uses of children). It had been then a mother-daughter family, with the father in the role of an outsider. However, the parents had never separated; they had wanted the girl to "know family life." Later knowledge and insight revealed that utter coldness between her parents, though it existed to a large degree, was exaggerated by the patient. It served her wish that the parents be divided so that she could be the sole object of her mother's attention. She then elaborated the fantasy of their sexual aloofness into a cold war between the sexes entailing the male's exclusion from the family constellation as much as possible. It was as if her mother had established a matriarchy to which she was heir and to which she owed her efforts and loyalty.

Now that the patient had children of her own, she was following her mother's example. Although it would be incorrect to say that sexual fears and taboos were not involved, her overriding motivation appeared to be her deep-rooted antagonism and hostility toward her husband. Her feelings were unrelated to any conscious personal grievance against her husband for something he had done but rested on the ground that he was the enemy as defined by the instructions of her mother or perhaps by her having to play the role of wife with him. She wanted to go one step beyond her mother: she hoped to eliminate her husband completely from the family constellation, thus proving to her daughters the strength, competence, and independence of the female sex.

It was only after the patient recognized this inherited ideal that she was able to contemplate certain alternative patterns of living. Up to this point she had deceived herself that she had some rare illness or affliction of which she was the helpless victim. She had wanted to see herself as too shy and timid to have a thought or conviction of her own. These defenses of self-effacement appeared to place her on the side of the angels, and they promoted a pleasing image not unlike that of the Virgin Mary, with whom she privately identified.

Perceiving that her husband was no different from other husbands in that he too was oblivious of her need for identity as a person, she was able to achieve a reconciliation with him of some warmth and affection. However, this did not come about until she established some autonomy. By good fortune she was able to get involved in an antipoverty program that interested her. Her relations with her husband improved only after she had confirmation of her worthiness in the external world.

The sexual withdrawal of the male from the female is seen less frequently but probably occurs as often as the reverse. For fairly obvious reasons a deprived wife is not likely to make the loud complaints that a husband would. She may have been taught that she should have no interest in sexual relations, and she has almost certainly been exposed to the myth of the male's sexual avidity, so that her husband's withdrawal indicates something wrong with *her*, not him. It is an unwise wife who casts any doubt on her husband's maleness.

In addition women are taught to key their sexual responses to the cues of their man and not to expect him to be reciprocally sensitive. Karen DeCrow describes this:

> This pleasing of men has sexual, in addition to social and intellectual, connotations. At one time we women were chaste, because men wanted wives to be chaste. The Victorian concept of two kinds of women—whores and wives—was well integrated into American mores. So, women didn't go to bed before marriage because *men wanted it that way*. More recently we have had the so-called sexual revolution. It is only so-called, because it has not changed the relations between the sexes at all. Men now want women who are great in bed. So, girls study up on how to be great in bed. Virginity is no longer what the men want (most of them); athletic and participating bed partners is what they want. So, women go to bed before marriage because *men want it that way*.
>
> Sexual freedom for women would mean, of course, that a woman could choose to be celibate, to sleep with one man, to sleep with many men—because *she wanted it that way*.[11]

Modern novels such as Bruce Jay Friedman's *A Mother's Kisses* portray women who are not at all quiet about their sex wants. Perhaps the type is increasing in society as well, but the overwhelming majority of women do not wish to announce publicly that their sex lives are inadequate. A woman who calls her husband inadequate may very well find herself labeled as a nymphomaniac, while a man may call his wife frigid and receive sympathy from all directions.

Traditionally and perhaps sadly sex has been encumbered by its use as a principal medium of social expression—most often of social discontent. Sex has always been a source of some power that a woman could wield over her husband, but perhaps this is less so today, when many options are open to him. Often a wife's negativism not only fails to achieve its goal but becomes counterproductive. For after a few rebuffs the husband may, in his cultivated and civilized manner, never "ask" her again. Otherwise contented with his family setup, he will not seek a legal separation or divorce but will seek his sexual gratification elsewhere—no beggar he. His wife then can make celibacy a virtue, try to reseduce him, or—rarely—seek her own sexual pleasure elsewhere.

His opportunities are far more numerous than hers, however, because he goes to an office every day. Sex is of course inevitable between people who work in continuous close contact. And in contrast to wives, who may visit hurts and denials on a man at home, secretaries can be inordinately attentive and understanding. There is also aid from the Internal Revenue Service, which makes the trip of an accompanying secretary tax-deductible while that of the wife often is not.

Office sex can of course cause trouble too. Robert Townsend relates an incident of a personnel vice-president who was generally very competent with bills and budgets but who found it difficult to finance an executive secretary in the firm with whom he had a sexual liaison. He tried to solve it in an altruistic but quixotic way that in the end cost him his head: he quietly raised the salaries of *all* the executive secretaries. Townsend fired him. The salaries of the executive secretaries were then cut back to the previous levels without a single protest from the temporary beneficiaries. If Townsend had not blown the whistle on the vice-president's generosity, the precedent of class benefit from individual action might have gained a foothold in American industry![12]

The real reason that people who work together often sleep together has nothing to do with tax deductibility. As people who have interesting careers have always known, work is very sexy, and the people with whom one is working are the people who excite. A day spent launching a project or writing a paper or running a seminar is more likely to stimulate—intellectually and sexually—than an evening spent sharing TV or discussing the lawn problems or going over the kids' report cards.

Wives know this, and it is a rare one who does not have anxious misgivings when her spouse takes a female coworker with him on a trip. The combination of their proximity, their common interest, and their distance from her makes it all too likely that business will spill over into pleasure.

The likelihood in fact provoked something close to mutiny among navy wives in August 1972, following a directive from the Chief of Naval Operations, Admiral Elmo R. Zumwalt, Jr., lifting the ban against women serving aboard warships at sea.[13] Apparently navy wives have been and are willing to endure long separations from their spouses, but a swarm of alarmed and outraged enlisted men's wives at Norfolk, Virginia, the world's largest naval community, collected several hundred signatures on petitions protesting "Z-gram No. 116." One woman is reported to have said, "I just don't think it's right they take our husbands away from us so many months at a time—and then put other women with them." Another saw navy ships turned into floating whorehouses. A third felt that having women aboard would put a cruel restraint on the men: "They're not going to be able to relax—they can't run around in their skivvies. . . ." Another wife lamented that the men would not be able to curse, adding: "When men go out to sea, they're animals. They live like animals."

Only one navy wife favored the new directive. Having formerly served in the navy herself, she regretted that she had not been allowed to go to sea. Now the wife of a hospital corpsman and the mother of two children, she totally disagreed with the other women about the horrors and injustice of having women aboard ships. She believed that women "should hold any shipboard rating that they are 'physically and mentally' qualified for." She vehemently resented the floating whorehouse image as an insult to herself as a former navy person and to people of both sexes who had jobs to do.

It is all too apparent that Z-gram No. 116 awakened lurid, close-to-the-surface sexual fantasies. Although matters of pride might make them reluctant to verbalize such a feeling, the navy wives seemed clearly to fear that shipboard romances might blossom and seriously disrupt family unity. On the other hand they appeared to believe that no such threats are apt to emanate from shore revels. Navy wives, accepting separations and loneliness as part of their lives, understandably don't take the prospect of being dumped lightly.

While in all probability the risk of being replaced by a seagoing woman is no greater than the danger of losing a husband to a land-based one, women working on ships might point up wives' own lives as agonizingly empty, passive, and ego-diminished by contrast. The jealousy of course has to surface in sexual terms, but it may in truth relate mainly to matters of status and identity. Although it may be true that they serve too who stand and wait, as of now no medals are being struck for such servers.

The corporate wife similarly will have to deal increasingly with the presence in their husbands' work lives of other women in greater numbers and at levels of competence and authority far beyond the present. Here too inevitably contrasts will surface between the active, achieving woman in the corporation and the corporate wife who, though enjoying secondary gains, must assume the passive and dependent role. For her neither are medals likely to be struck.

What will be the effects on corporate wives of the appearance of women executives? What is it to be like when men are surrounded by highly educated women with power and money? Will dutiful Jane at home be able to compete with her rising executive sister?

In the past executive women have posed no competitive threat to wives because there have barely *been* any. And the general description husbands have given their wives of the few who have made it has always been most reassuring, leaving no cause for suspicion or anxiety. The husband would tell about the woman engineer at the plant: what a freak—mannish, unattractive, no sex appeal. The threat has been from the ubiquitous secretaries whose job it is to serve executives in a hundred ways and who become very attractive for their unstinting cooperation, loyalty, and devotion.

It has been characteristic for men to love women who serve them. Since our culture defines "masculinity" in conjunction with aggression and control, even sexual pleasure often loses its appeal to men if their women do not serve and submit. Traditionally the imperative of the woman's diminution in the conjugal union has gone largely unquestioned. Men "love" (and often sleep with) their secretaries because these women serve them well and often intelligently, not only bringing the Danish pastry but also writing speeches and reports without byline. Excluded from the relationship at the office are the many gripes, financial problems, and children's sicknesses.

As corporate wives know, the secretary, or "office wife," is a hard act to follow. The office structure, typified by the male-boss/female-secretary dyad, is one of the impregnable bastions of sexism. The corporate wife and the office secretary, supposedly rivals and competitors, are often, as one might surmise, sister-victims.

131

ROOM AT THE TOP—
FOR MEN ONLY

> *Things are looking up. You don't hear
> about the company "Nigger" much any-
> more, and the company "Kike" is now the
> company Jew. Women are still bottom-of-
> the-heap. "Don't give her a raise; she's
> making a lot for a woman."*
>
> ROBERT TOWNSEND

A FEW YEARS AGO the *Harvard Business Review* attempted to survey
executive opportunities for women. The editors gave up in despair because there was nothing to study. Despite the fact that there were then
30 million working women in the labor force, at the top—the executive,
decision-making levels—practically none were to be found.

In 1972 Dr. Margaret Henning, of Simmons College, found barely
enough to make a study. In all of corporate America, she was able to
locate only 110 women who had gained top management positions outside the traditionally female fields.[1]

Today economists estimate that 94 percent of jobs paying more than
$15,000 are in the control of white males.

It seems inconceivable that in the future women will be shut out as
they have been in the past. The new militancy, with its demands for
justice and fair play, appears undaunted. The myth of male superiority
and supremacy will increasingly disappear for all except the naive or
the ruthless. Similarly the rigid sex roles, with their simplistic concepts
of masculinity and femininity, will no longer constitute definitions of
male and female. For it is human intelligence, not physical force, that
runs the world as well as corporations; there is no scientific or psychological study that can be brought forth to indicate that women are inferior to men in intelligence.

A discussion of this subject by syndicated columnist Sylvia Porter is most instructive. "Aptitude tests," she writes, "have repeatedly shown that women can perform just about any job as well as men can. Women are now represented in every one of the 400 plus occupations listed in the 1970 census. Yet, in defiance of all equal opportunity laws, job labeling persists—and it continues to bar women from the higher-level, higher-paying jobs."[2] Ms. Porter then debunks a number of current myths:

1. *Women are absent from their jobs because of illness more than men.*

The truth is that the absenteeism rates for men and women are about the same though women are absent more often from high managerial positions that have always been associated with lower absenteeism. If the overall figure is weighted for this factor, absenteeism among women is probably lower than among men.

2. *Women switch jobs more than men.*

The job-changing rate is slightly higher for women, but men are more likely to change occupations than women.

3. *In this high-unemployment period, women are taking jobs away from men, the traditional breadwinners.*

In 1971 there was an average of 18.5 million married women in the labor force as compared with 3 million unemployed men. Thus if all the women had quit and the 3 million unemployed men had taken their vacated jobs, there would have been 15.5 million unfilled jobs, which would have created an economic disaster. And few of the unemployed 3 million men had the education and skills to fill the jobs held by women.

4. *Women work only for pin money.*

About four out of five women who work do so because they must. According to the U.S. Dept. of Labor Women's Bureau, of the 33 million women in the workforce 17 percent are widowed, divorced, or separated and 23 percent are single. Another 30 percent have husbands whose annual income is below $7,000.

5. *Training women is a waste of money since they quit when they marry or have children.*

In fact the separations from jobs are temporary. Taking into account the time for child bearing and rearing, the work-life expectancy for the American woman is 25 years. For a single woman it is 45 years, in contrast to the overall average of 43 years for men, married or single.

6. *Men don't like to work for women.*

According to the Department of Labor's Women's Bureau, "Most men who complain about women supervisors never worked for a woman."

7. *Women fall apart in a crisis.*

To answer this Ms. Porter quotes Charles D. Orth, a career development specialist: "If men are present during a crisis, they expect the women involved to become emotional and fall apart—and women often do oblige. But somehow, if men are absent, women usually cope quite well."

In order for women to hold high positions, no intellectual or educational concessions need be made, as have been proposed for other underrepresented groups. Women can compete without special favors or advantages if the opportunities are presented. The era of passive acceptance of inequality as well as feminine obeisance is rapidly coming to an end. While it is true that the majority of women, like any majority, has been slow to join in protests and boycotts, there is growing evidence (for example the national political conventions) that women from many spheres are beginning to demand equality.

With the change in national mood and the elimination of legal and statutory encumbrances, more women will become corporate leaders. Pressure from consumer-interest groups, customers, and stockholders will increase to make companies aware of unequal employment practices. For instance women corporate executives will have to be visible at annual meetings in the future. Women do hold a goodly amount of stock shares, and they will increasingly demand that their sex be fairly represented on executive committees and boards of directors. Moreover company officials as well as Madison Avenue experts are well aware of how much purchasing power women exercise. The pressure of a boycott against a corporation that discriminates against women in its hiring policies will dramatically change attitudes heretofore considered impregnable.

The pressure is coming from a broader sector than the Women's Liberation groups. The courts are consistently deciding for women employees in suits charging unfair employment practices. Government agencies, under the mandates of Executive Orders 11375 and 11246 of the 1960s and the tougher Order No. 4 of 1970, can and do revoke contracts if the companies do not take affirmative action to treat women equally in their workforce. And affirmative action requires more than simply giving equal pay to women currently working for the firm (no small change in itself) and promoting them according to merit; it requires that the companies actively recruit and train women for executive positions. The specter of severe financial penalties and loss of government contracts may prick the conscience of many a corporate king.

It is the new federal regulation—Revised Order No. 4, which went into effect in April 1972—that has precipitated the sexual crisis in corporate America. It establishes the "right of women to advance to executive and managerial levels in business organizations." The order affects all companies holding government contracts that have 50 or more employees or do contract business in excess of $50,000 a year, and it includes a requirement of periodic audits. Women for the first time are covered under the equal employment opportunity program that has worked to some extent for other disadvantaged segments of the labor market.

Executive Order 4 has been the impetus for much corporate committee work, much hiring of consultants, and probably much head shaking. As of this writing it is too early to determine whether its stipulations will be effectively implemented or circumvented. We do know that Women's Liberation groups will keep a sharp eye on both implementation and enforcement. It must be noted that this order emanated from the Nixon administration, which is both conservative and not particularly committed to women's rights. This is strong validation of the thesis that the inclusion of women at all levels of decision making in business as well as government is an issue whose time has come.

American industry is gearing up for this transformation. An increasing number of companies are expanding facilities (not just restrooms) to accommodate working women and mothers. Some—among them the Bell System—are establishing and contributing to childcare centers for offspring of both male and female employees. Each passing day brings to light more evidence that corporate America is accepting its mothers, sisters, and daughters to its bosom—a switch long overdue.

Moving well ahead of Executive Order 4, International Business Machines Corporation has tripled the number of women managers since 1967 in response to internal enlightenment as well as prescience of things to come. Boise Cascade has rewritten its employment application deleting all questions about marital status, number of dependents, and employment of spouse. The major auto companies now allow women on maternity leave to collect six weeks' pay. The first paternity leave has been written into a labor agreement: the City University of New York will now give fathers paid leave to take care of their young children, which equalizes both parental responsibility and the anticipated burdens the employer faces in dealing with men and women workers.

Among the few women who have reached the top of the corporate ladders, Catherine B. Cleary, the first and only woman on the board of the American Telephone & Telegraph Company, was similarly elected the first and only woman on the board of the world's largest corporation, General Motors, in October 1972. Although cynics may say that this is tokenism—that corporate America has found its "safe" woman

135

and keeps using her for display purposes—having her up there constitutes progress whatever the shortcomings. If it does nothing more than desegregate in appearance only the most powerful male club in the world, an important step has been achieved.

The Bell System, which was called "without doubt the largest oppressor of women workers in the United States" by the Equal Employment Opportunity Commission, agreed in September 1972 that it would change its ways.[3] Following a year of negotiations with the General Services Administration, AT&T said that its 21 operating units would provide more than 50,000 higher-paying jobs for women, 10 percent of them at management levels. In entry-level jobs some 6,600 women would be hired into previously male positions, as telephone installers for example, and 4,000 men would be used in traditionally female jobs, as operators for instance.

But this was not the last word. The Department of Labor's Office of Federal Contract Compliance was dissatisfied with the plan agreed to by the GSA. So were women's rights and minority groups, which attacked the agreement as inadequate. Labor unions on the other hand complained that it interfered with the seniority and transfer provisions of their contracts.[4] AT&T thus found itself unable to expiate its sins even when it had laid itself bare on the altar.

This situation illustrates once again that the women's struggle, like many others, is not a battle of good against evil but a conflict of diverse forms each of which has a legitimate claim to be heard. As much as we need and enjoy their presence (to appear as saints by contrast), real devils these days are hard to find.

But if real devils are hard to find, so is a good woman, according to the headline of a news story in *The New York Times*. Reporter Marylin Bender quotes a vice-president of one of the better-known executive search firms as lamenting, "Can you tell me where we can look for ladies? We never looked for ladies before."[5]

Executive Order 4 has set corporate executives to finding women for executive jobs. Many industries are embarking on education programs to prepare their personnel for the change, realizing that the male executive—who has learned *machismo* from early childhood—will likely find it difficult to work side by side with women as equals and, especially, to work under a woman boss. IBM for instance requires all its managers to attend a three-hour program on sex bias using a $50,000 film as a visual aid. The film describes the frustrations and struggles as well as the ongoing sex-labeled myths that may plague the woman attempting a business career. Equality will undoubtedly come as a bitter pill to

136

the unliberated. It will prove a harsh test for men who are able to "love" only those women who are invisible or inferior.

Experts and business organizations are being consulted as never before. The American Management Associations ran its first Women in Management Conference in May 1972, and many others are planned. A score or more of similar activities have sprung up, many in connection with women's rights organizations, principally the National Organization for Women (NOW).

AMR International Inc., a New York concern that provides advanced training for business executives, reports a great demand for its new management-skills seminar for women. Katherine Gibbs School has also begun offering evening management courses for women. In fact the influx of women into management has given rise to a new breed of consultant to train women executives. The demand for services is so great that a principal worry is that opportunists may appear to exploit the need.

On September 28, 1972, a conference called "A Career Encounter" in New York City brought together representatives of 22 major American corporations and 247 women, all college graduates with business experience.[6] The object of the meeting was the recruitment of talented women for executive positions. Management executives were counseled in techniques of recruitment for jobs as diverse as production supervision, finance, and administration. Recruiters were "warned not to refer to the women as girls, ladies, or gals and to avoid such clichés as 'vive la différence.' They were also advised not to be prejudiced to women who had been school teachers or social workers and wanted to get into marketing and sales."

Although workshops and courses can do much to motivate and inspire women, they may stir expectations that, for the time being at least, the business world is unprepared and unwilling to meet. "In some cases, companies send women to management-development courses just to quiet them down," says Charles D. Orth, president of Career Development International Inc., a consulting firm that provides career guidance for businesswomen. As a result, most consultants believe that attitudes of men, as well as women, must change before equal opportunity programs can work. Rosalind Loring, of UCLA, says, "If I had my druthers, I'd plan all my courses for men on how to work with women."

A woman in a predominantly male training course may be patronized and intimidated so that she can't participate actively. Even if she wants to, she may find her efforts consistently resisted by the men.

In an effort to see that consulting truly does help women, the Association of Feminist Consultants was founded. It is an association for independent feminist consultants engaged in the business of providing industry, government, educational, and nonprofit organizations with professional management consulting services aimed at improving the economic and social status of women. Coordinated by Dr. Jennifer Macleod, of Princeton Junction, New Jersey, the AFC's purpose is to establish and maintain professional standards, to exchange information, and to promote the advantages of employing qualified experts on feminist issues when initiating or implementing programs and practices concerned with changing the role of women in society.

One of the last bastions of male exclusiveness is that of sales. Now this too is crumbling as women are being hired and found to be quite successful. Philip H. Dougherty, who writes a daily column about the advertising business, reports that *Newsweek* and *Time* have added women to their advertising sales staffs, as has *American Home* magazine. Many corporations report that although they originally hired women as an expedient, "We have been nothing but satisfied." Arthur Pardoll, of Foote, Cone & Belding, is quoted as saying, "The top female salesman will match the best male salesman in ability. They don't rely heavily on their charms although a number of them could." Warren Bahr, of Young & Rubicam, says, "They sell differently. They deliver the message more earnestly, stick to the script and work harder at it. They have less tendency to chat away from the subject. They make real sales calls."[7] These statements contrast sharply with the usual biased characterizations about women we are accustomed to hearing: that they are chatterboxes, unreliable, and lazy.

These are small, first steps that we are witnessing in our era. For the first time government is interceding to promote justice and fair play for women in employment. Predictably there will be much foot dragging and token compliance. Before using the drastic penalty of contract revocation, the government will hold hearings and attempt to settle matters through "conciliation, mediation, and persuasion." Inevitably, however, many cases will be brought to the courts, where delays and appeals may forestall implementation for years. In the process many women will grow discouraged and drop their claims. Others will become over-age and retire.

Entering high-level employment successfully entails much more than opportunity, enthusiasm, and goodwill for a woman. If she is married she will be faced with handling a new creature on the domestic front— the corporate husband. Will he be able to withstand the fantasy (or reality) of being "cuckolded" by his wife for another interest that takes her away from him? Will he feel comfortable about her missing dinner for that evening meeting or being absent for days on an important business trip or convention? And what will happen when a company has to transfer a female executive from one city to another? At an IBM Awareness Session sponsored by Barbara Boyle and Sharon Kirkman, consultants to business in affirmative action programs, an executive stated that he would not offer a job requiring geographic relocation to a woman "before he had consulted her husband." Miss Boyle responded by asking the executive, who had already moved five times for the corporation, whether *his* wife would be called first if another move was in the offing. "Oh, no," he protested. "She'd never agree." Miss Boyle suggested that "awareness" had been achieved.[8]

The sense of male privilege and priority has become so much a part of men's mentality (and secondarily many women's) that it has obliterated basic egalitarian considerations even among the well-educated. They fail even to hear how bad it sounds.

A woman worker faces other and subtler difficulties, usually stemming from centuries of sexist mores and practices, that are largely solved for the man by custom and consent. Regrettably, in order to succeed today, women must be more capable and quick on their feet than their male counterparts. Most women show great tact in dealing with these problems.

An example is who pays for lunch. If the woman does she generally offends the chivalry of male customers. Suzanne Douglas Brennan, working on sales for *Sports Illustrated* and *Time,* has made arrangements with 10 restaurants and a country club to be billed so that no check is brought to the table. She relates that at one time this situation bothered some men, but later they laughed about it, muttering, "It's nice to be kept." Someday men will have the strength of character to be gracious guests of women without feeling a sense of humiliation. Actually it isn't nice to be kept—it is degrading and dehumanizing to be a perpetual recipient of another's generosity, as men intuitively know. The brilliant philosopher Sören Kierkegaard wrote, expanding on the Biblical dictum, that it is better to give than to receive—and it is far more difficult to receive than to give.

The woman who seeks a professional identity in the world is thus faced with many hazards, and they do not arise only from a hostile and resentful environment. She may also be thrown off balance by inner doubts about what she is doing. Even when she reassures herself or is given support that her stand is proper and justified, she frequently manifests a feeling of guilt about not being in her proper place, the home, distorting her character into grotesque shapes.

Dr. Matina Horner, University of Michigan social scientist who is now president of Radcliffe, has uncovered a root of this problem. She discovered that 75 percent of women entering the business world felt threatened with unpopularity, loneliness, guilt, and loss of womanhood as they found themselves competing with men. Striving for worldly success is apparently deemed such an exclusively masculine trait that women have a built-in motive to avoid achievement. Dr. Horner's studies thus reveal still another double standard: women are taught to fear success as much as men are conditioned to abhor failure.[9]

As an increasing number of women are given executive responsibilities, many will fall on their faces, and others will cut and run—casualties of stereotypic indoctrination in the formative years. Their failures will be welcomed and broadly advertised by those who need rationalizations for misogyny. It is well to forewarn both women and prospective employers of some of the pitfalls. A job is not a treatment for emotional problems. When it is used as such, disappointment and frustration result. There are instances where a job has proved disastrous to a woman who has pinned her hope on it as a way of solving complex problems of living. Particularly for women who have been out of the job market for a decade or two, the reentry hazards are formidable.

A woman who fears success more than failure may cover her many anxieties with a disturbing aggressivity that makes productive work relationships very difficult. She may appear not so much mannish as apish. She constantly seeks to prove—and usually finds—that she is being unfairly treated. She may then divert most of her energies and time to a personal civil rights issue, making herself an anathema in the office and generally earning loathing from coworkers who otherwise might accept her talents. She is soon diagnosed as not really committed to her work but primarily interested in a life-and-death struggle with men. This type frequently earns a male backlash that hurts all womankind: the men reaffirm their basic prejudice that women belong in the home.

Behind the facade of bravado, these women are usually very fearful of their new roles and overreact. Their difficulty adjusting and their perpetual grievance hunting contain a hidden appeal to be sent back to the kitchen, from which their liberation has been specious. Undertones of this were audible in the following case.[10]

A 24-year-old woman, a graduate of a school of engineering, became a junior executive in an industrial firm. Her attitude was that she would neither ask nor give any quarter. She was most serious in every project she undertook, brooked no levity, and resented any flirtatiousness, though she was quite attractive in spite of her austere manner. No slight, real or fancied, passed her by. When invitations were sent to "employees and their wives" for company social affairs, she would reply with a long and biting letter that this was the twentieth century and that routine form letters had to be altered to acknowledge the existence of female employees. She studied the salary scales of the men and women and brought the inevitable inequities under the nose of her employer. She also ranted about the inefficiencies and stupidities of the men around her and accused them of having little interest in their jobs except for the pay checks and automatic promotions involved. Her general behavior made her male associates very happy with their own wives—she brought a ray of darkness into their working lives that made their home lives seem that much brighter. She was married, but she disdained anything about her own home and had made an agreement with her husband that there would be no children until she was well along in her career.

In time she came into heated controversy over policies with her boss. She threatened to go to the stockholders about the terrible state management was in. She was fired in this clash of personalities. Although her competence was never in question, her adaptability was zero.

After her dismissal she became distraught. For a while she railed against her former employer, against men in general, and against a civilization that sanctioned injustices. But she lost interest in work, as if she had been badly injured, and made no attempt to find other employment. Instead she preferred to stay at home and lick her wounds, and she withdrew into herself.

Her condition of distress manifested itself now in severe phobic reactions: if she tried to cross the threshold of her front door, she was stopped by feelings of dread; she was too fearful to answer the doorbell or the telephone. She became completely housebound, needed the constant presence of her husband, and was obsessed with losing her mind. Her husband had to do all the shopping and communicating with the outside world.

Here was a transformation of a person as complete as could be imagined. People who had known her in her former state of independence and arrogance could not recognize her now. They postulated that either she had been undone by injustice—a man in her job might have been treated with more respect and listened to more tolerantly—or her aggressive behavior had been a manifestation of an incipient mental illness.

This point is indeed difficult to decide. No one could ever say that extreme frustration and disappointment could not destroy a person. Yet her attitude was such that she ignored the need for adaptation. Who would find her wrong in wanting equality, acting directly, and not submitting to the circuitous and hypocritical modes of behavior that are expected of inferiors? In defense of her employer, it may be assumed that he had felt a personal sense of nobility in hiring her against the advice of others who worried about allowing a woman to enter the managerial level. He would then have looked on himself as her benefactor and expected her gratitude and loyalty if not obeisance. Instead he got the opposite and had to suffer the humiliation of her attacks and his confreres' smiles.

Another type, equally insecure, is the woman who must exaggerate her femininity in the so-called masculine world. She wants to do a reasonably successful job but runs from any hint of competition with men. She dresses consciously in a conventionally feminine fashion, usually on the sexy side. She takes every opportunity to appear helpless, and she never relinquishes the niceties traditionally due a woman according to etiquette. Unlike the woman just described, she overlooks inequities and tries to defer to men as much as possible. At critical points she appeals to their strength, and if pressed she may proclaim that line of Americana, "But I'm only a woman!"

In line with this posture is her vulnerability to the reawakening of the adolescent crush syndrome—falling in love with a man she is working with who has given her aid or has promoted her cause in the office over the resistance of others. He then appears as her true knight in armor, performing the rescue mission she has always dreamed of. In this he eclipses her husband, who is usually in no position to promote her career in more than a passive way. Her enthrallment with her new benefactor may lead to fantasied or actual extramarital activities that may wreck her household. In her anxieties about her new role, she reacts with imprudence and may destroy both her home life and her career.

This hazard was illustrated by a 36-year-old woman, mother of three, who decided to return to her field, experimental psychology, after 14 years of marriage and professional inactivity. She felt that her children no longer needed as much care as formerly and that she could profitably pick up her career. She returned to work on a part-time basis with the general approval of her family. She was filled with enthusiasm and hope, despite the many years she had been away from her field.

Being an affable and attractive person, she was well received in the laboratory. She was given extensive briefings by coworkers and was praised for her enthusiasm if not competence. She was a delight to have around because of her good nature. She expressed her gratitude frequently and asked that her shortcomings be tolerated until she could learn the required techniques.

She came under the tutelage and supervision of a senior male psychologist, who appeared especially attracted to her. He patiently introduced her to new methods in the field, and they set up a research project. Through their work as a research team, or partnership as they preferred to call it, she attained a degree of competence that led to her having several scientific papers published. She began to become known in her field.

Her husband and children joined her in the pleasure of her accomplishments and continued to encourage her in her pursuits. His benevolent attitude had afforded her the opportunity to achieve in her field. But while seemingly she still loved him, his role was eclipsed by the active help that the senior psychologist gave her. In the course of two years at work, she developed feelings of deep love for her research partner. He on the other hand felt great affection for her but never moved to indicate that he desired a relationship beyond a friendly professional one.

Meanwhile his work had become highly thought of, and he was offered a chair at a leading university, which he accepted. On learning of this she was to all appearances joyful over his good fortune, but privately she became despondent. Her life and personal success had been intimately tied to him and his presence. He had been her rescuer and was about to desert her. She had no confidence that she could function on her own or could cooperate with the others in the laboratory without his kindly intervention. Her despondence became overt: she could no longer tolerate her husband or her children, and she felt now that she had been victimized but did not know her oppressor. In her depressed state she attempted suicide, but she was saved by her thoroughly perplexed husband. No longer able to work or to relate to her family, she asked to be hospitalized. Her adventure had brought ruin on herself and her loved ones.

Who or what was at fault? The husband for being cooperative? She for wanting to pursue her career? The psychologist for wanting to be a helpful friend? Let the reader decide. It was my personal impression that the fault belonged to no one of them and yet a little to all. Unpreparedness, imprudence, and lack of perspective were the predominant shortcomings.

The suddenness of her success and the strangeness of the professional environment clouded her judgment and threw her value system out of balance. Her freedom was a fresh, new penny, and she became pennyfoolish, to the distress of all. Yet this evident failure in no way proves a basic weakness in women or the appropriateness of this or that role. Rather it should point up the complexities and challenges of women's struggle for intellectual survival. This woman suffered culture shock;

hers was a problem of reentry no less difficult than that encountered in space exploration.

Failures such as those described in these two cases, and they are frequent, become living ammunition for people who preach that professional roles are unnatural for women; much is always made of the mess they create in any but their divinely appointed life of domesticity. For the patient observer these instances, far from proving female inferiority or biological or divine determinism, merely testify to the inherent problems of transition, the period in any new human venture when both sides are unsure that what they are doing is right. They then are apt to overreact, feel themselves fools, and swear, "Never again." This is unwarranted pessimism, as the history of social advances demonstrates. These problems will eventually be resolved as both sexes accommodate themselves to new and more equitable modes of behavior.

The transition period is not likely to be short; women have always had the capacity and have in general developed the skills to fill higher-level posts than have been open to them in business and public life. They have been until recently unable to break through the lower echelons regardless of education, training, and experience. Visible to the world in outside offices—as tellers, information suppliers, counter personnel—they are not to be found elsewhere.

Perhaps the most widespread example of the discrepancy between ability and authority is the case of the secretary. She typically must promote the ambitions of others but must abjure any such hopes herself. For years she may train new, young executives to go on to bigger and better things, knowing that though she will get small increments in pay, she will herself never be elevated to executive status. She keeps her boss in the public eye but shields him from his own underlings. She on the other hand is highly visible to the company personnel but anonymous in most of the work she performs. All credit accrues to her boss, whether she writes a memo for him or arranges an important meeting.

Jack Olsen has described the plight of secretaries in *The Girls in the Office*,[11] the "girls" being 15 women working for an elite American corporation who are brutalized by servile roles that border on masochism. Starting careers with some hope for personal growth, they soon find that there is a withering of identity. They have no real recognition and often serve as mere decorations. Those who have some meaningful work perpetually remain "assistants," even when they do the job of a disabled or incompetent boss. And as if to make the subservience and anonymity complete, there is habitual secret pairing with the married men, whether in hotel rooms rented at noon or in evening liaisons following office parties. The women maintain the hope of marrying and having children, consonant with societal expectations and their own lack of promising careers, but this rarely comes. Being smiling, cheerful, and subservient "girls" doesn't pay off either professionally or socially.

"Assistant" is widely used in organizations to keep competent women mollified. But a title doesn't substitute for true standing. A talented assistant professor of English at a prestigious Eastern university told of her chagrin over her position. Always praised for her work, she would be respectfully consulted whenever an appointment to a high office was to be made, a new chairman appointed, or a committee formed to search for a new dean. The men in the department would look—as she related it—straight at her and ask who she thought would be a good person for the job. They always meant a good man. It never occurred to them that *she* might be the person for a higher position. She had the feeling that they would be astonished that she too had desires for elevation. When her disappointment about constantly being overlooked—in effect looked through—became known, her male colleagues stated that she was already doing pretty well "for a woman."

Another instance of a woman "assistant" came to my attention a few years ago. An attractive, primly dressed 32-year-old married woman was referred to me for therapy. She complained of being tired and listless, of lacking in energy. At times she would burst into tears without apparent reason. She was dissatisfied with her husband, who was now beginning to withdraw from her. Married for 10 years they had no children by mutual agreement. She had been repeatedly examined by competent physicians, who had found no physical cause for her distress. One doctor volunteered the suggestion that perhaps she should quit work and have a child—she might be unfulfilled in that area. She would hear none of this.

In the course of therapy, it became evident that unhappiness with her job was a major contributor to her distress, though she was unable in the beginning to perceive or articulate a cause-and-effect relationship. At the age of 19, she had gone to work for a major multinational corporation. With a high school diploma and one year of college, she had at first been assigned to a stenographic pool. After four years she had been promoted to the job of secretary to three young executives. The work was interesting, and she had been delighted with the change.

Because she was affable and attractive, she received compliments from most of the men she worked for. And because her section had had the responsibility for a popular new product, business had boomed. She had worked overtime and had received increases in salary. Although always the "assistant," she had taken on major management responsibilities as well as the indoctrination and training of a flow of young men

145

just out of college who were on their way to managerial positions. Mary was dependable. She knew where everything was and how to get things done. Within two days even the newest executive recruit knew her as "Mary." Some sexual advances had been made, but these had never been a problem.

Finally, after a shift, she had only one boss, who found her indispensable. He would often assign her the task of writing his speeches, memos, and even articles for trade journals. And she shielded him from the burdensome routine requests of other officials and departments. The section had grown to a division, and her boss had received a series of promotions in both status and money. Mary's rewards had been exclusively monetary, but even these had never been commensurate with her contributions to the company.

As in the instance of the woman faculty member described earlier, her boss would consult her about whom to put into a new or vacated supervisory job. She would dutifully concur with his opinion or make recommendations of her own, which he would consider seriously. It had become known that Mary was indeed very influential and a good person to impress or cultivate.

Her boss never failed to *listen* to her, but he never was able or willing to *see* her. When she at one point had meekly suggested that she might be good at a certain job, he had squeezed her affectionately and sighed, "And what would I do without you?" She had never brought the subject up with him again. However, she had made informal inquiries with the director of personnel about her chances for moving into an executive position. At first surprised, he had then told of the difficulties and obstacles in the way of a person without a college degree. It was company policy that college graduates were brought in through one door with certain expectations for the future and noncollege people through another. Inside the company the segregation continued without breach. The director had gone on to make it clear that she was considered one of the firm's top nonexecutive people.

It was in this setting that Mary's enthusiasm had begun to waiver, though she had continued to function as well as she could. Then her distressing physical symptoms had appeared. Much of her disappointment she had kept hidden even from herself lest she be deemed ungrateful, selfish, or "ambitious." She had taken pride in her femininity, never identifying herself with those strident women who took to the streets with placards. And yet the thankless experience of training and teaching others with no prospect of achieving status for herself had finally dispirited her.

During therapy, which lasted three years, she was able to come to grips with her hidden feelings of frustration and resentment. And she came to see that her desires were not abnormal or selfish but valid expectations for any person brought up on the American credo that hard work is the proper way of getting ahead. She saw finally that it is proper for a woman, a thoroughly feminine woman, to want to get ahead.

The main success of the therapy was that it served as a catalyst for action. While working at her job, despite deep apprehensions, she began to take college courses at night. Characteristically she received *A*'s in all her class work. She is well on her way toward completion. And because of bitter memories and personal disappointments, once armed with her degree, she is going to try her luck anew with another company—this time hopefully through the right door.

Unfortunately the outcome in Mary's case is exceptional. Most women drag on with neither protest nor promotion. And there is no guarantee, even with presidential orders for equal opportunity, that Mary will be able to achieve advances consonant with her capabilities.

An increasing number of women are returning to school, either to complete a degree interrupted by marriage or to earn an advanced degree to qualify for professional or academic work. Many husbands are encouraging their wives to continue or resume their education as a means of insuring the financial security of the family in case anything should happen to them. For families that cannot afford adequate insurance, the earning capability of the wife is indispensable to the future security of the family.

Journalist Olive Evans also writes of women who return to school.[12] As could be anticipated, all is not a bed of roses. Those who are aiming to teach find few openings in the area of their specialty. Their lack of mobility makes the situation even harder. And women in their 50s are met with statements like "Why aren't you home being a nice grandmother?"

With all the struggle for training, women ruefully predict, they will return to where they started from. "There are many of us. And what's going to happen? They're going to end up as secretaries. And they'll know that they're smarter than their bosses and can write a better letter and they won't dare to put Ph.D. down on the application form because if they did they wouldn't get the job." So we come full circle: the woman, frustrated at her secretarial job, returning to school to equip herself for better things as personnel directors insist she must, and then having to hide her training to make a living—as a secretary.

This suppression has its cost in discontentment and rage that are not confined to the psychiatrist's purview. Being able and prepared but always being overlooked for advancement, as women in business are, creates a special despair unknown to other "minority" groups. For unlike others, women as a whole lack no education, are deficient in no skills, never score lower on intelligence or aptitude tests, have no criminal records, are impeccably patriotic, are not prone to absenteeism, and write, read, and speak the language without fault. In short they are well outside the stereotyped rationalizations that have kept the disadvantaged from rising. Women do not even have the luxury of being given a reasonable excuse for their exclusion. In such instances knowledge of one's deficiency can serve psychologically to explain one's lack of progress. There may be little consolation in knowing that one *is* lacking in preparation, but there is no consolation at all in knowing that one is not unprepared but is perpetually treated as such. It does not take a great psychologist to predict that there is going to be an increasing number of enraged women—there is nothing quite so disturbing as failing after you've done all the right things.

When employers have the will to free themselves from bias against women, many types of mutually advantageous accommodations can be made. Companies are finding a gold mine in untapped talent among well-educated women hired on a part-time basis. These women are able to work five-hour shifts and have been put to the test in a diversity of jobs. The fears that there would be poor adjustment or motivation and a high rate of absenteeism have been dispelled. The picture is just the opposite: employers are finding these women to be more productive than full-time staff. Allan Kullen, vice-president of the United Publishing Corp., a firm that has pioneered in short-shift employment of women, says: "I prefer working with part-time women. The mind doesn't have to be in an office 40 hours a week to be creative, and many women seem to put in a lot more time thinking about their job than the number of hours they get paid for." And the practical mentality of Mr. Kullen observes further, "The company doesn't have to pay fringe benefits to part-timers; these usually lift labor costs by at least 6 percent above salaries."[13]

The evidence for the feasibility of part-time work for women (and perhaps men too) is mounting. Carol Greenwald, a Federal Reserve economist herself, said at the Fourteenth Annual Meeting of the National Association of Business Economists, "By creating more part-time jobs . . . , [business] could recruit women of exceptional ability, reduce absenteeism, cut overtime costs and increase efficiency." Ms. Greenwald, mother of a small daughter, works a 20-hour week instead of the standard for her bank of 36 hours, and she receives five-ninths of her former salary.

Ms. Greenwald contends that various advantages accrue to management from this arrangement. She works harder: "You never get coffee breaks, you never have time to sit around and talk to friends." Moreover "Productivity will also rise because one can keep up a much faster pace for four hours a day than one can for eight hours." In addition, "Because women are so desirous of good part-time jobs, they will ideally assist [in] other changes that management may want to make but which they might resist strongly under other circumstances."[14]

These are attractive prospects; certainly an increasing number of women will press for similar arrangements. Short-shift work is an issue that cannot be hidden under the corporate carpet for long. Greater breakthroughs will occur as traditional attitudes and operating methods loosen. Already the Kellogg, Ford, and Rockefeller Foundations have allotted grants totaling $300,000 to draw up a program for the employment of well-educated women on less than a full-time basis.

Of course one can anticipate resistance to short-shift employment from several quarters. Many companies will not find the arguments in its favor convincing. They will evoke the specter of women being called away at inopportune times by a sick child or husband, and they will cite the inconvenience to full-time staff of scheduling shorter hours for some.

Granted, part-time employment for a fully capable person might seem a gross inequity to the more militant feminists. And it is. But as the sage said, half a loaf might be better than none. Furthermore, whether responding to reality or to guilt, many women feel threatened by full-time employment, especially when they have a young husband or young children. It is likely too that part-time work will in many instances graduate to full-time as women's domestic obligations lessen with the increasing independence of their children or the decreasing resistance of their husbands.

Even if management heroically accedes to this innovation, the labor unions will undoubtedly be heard from. Full-time employees might feel threatened indeed by an influx of grateful working women who indicate that they try harder and will be most cooperative with the boss. In many instances management will undoubtedly find that part-time help does as much as full-time for the reasons Ms. Greenwald related. Probably neither management nor labor wants to find this out.

Countering the resistance, interestingly enough, is the testimony of husbands who have overcome their chauvinism and are pleased with the results at home. They have come to realize that women aren't working part-time to help support the family, which might threaten the image of the husband as big-shot provider, but because "Work is simply an important part of their lives." Jim Malaro, a physicist at the Atomic Energy Commission, made this comment on the part-time work of his lawyer-wife: "I think it's great. Working has improved my wife's frame

149

of mind quite a bit. And it's good for the children not to depend on her all the time."[13]

Working part-time is becoming increasingly popular for men as well as women. Legislation was introduced in the House and the Senate in 1973 to provide that a certain percentage of federal civil service jobs—clerical as well as professional—be made available on a part-time basis. The legislation was originally designed to enable women (who still have the primary responsibility for child rearing) to enter the federal civil service, but it can be a liberating piece of legislation for men as well. Freed from the compulsions of working constantly, men can enhance their lives in whatever ways appeal to them.

The addition of women to the executive councils can bring new ideas and life to stagnant, inbred firms and may indeed save some from going under. John Naisbett, of the Urban Research Corp., has aptly remarked, "Too many executives see this as a compliance problem [with the executive orders], instead of seeing it as an opportunity to draw from this extraordinary talented labor pool in ways that for the first time are socially acceptable, even if not corporately acceptable."[15] In other words corporate executives may now feel forced into doing themselves a great favor.

Although we should not depend on Madison Avenue advertising writers for the whole truth about either the present or the future of our American culture, they are indeed shrewder than most in detecting shifts in the wind. And they are making preparations for the market of women executives. An ad appeared in several nationwide magazines in the summer of 1972 that showed a man placing a diamond necklace on a delighted woman. The copy read: "My first reaction was no wife of mine is going to work. But you taught me how wrong I was. And made me proud of you. Congratulations, darling, to the loveliest and best vice president ever promoted. And the best wife a man ever had." This is in sharp contrast to former ads for diamonds where the reward was for being solely "the best wife."

Women in the executive suite will of course be good for women—money and power are useful commodities in our society. Women in the executive suite will probably be good for children—relieving them of having to perform to satisfy the unrealized and displaced ambitions of their full-time mother. And women in the executive suite will be good for men—now burdened both materially and psychologically with supplying the full financial support of families. When men can relax about who rules the executive suite, they may indeed be able to relax in their demands on themselves to be strong and dominant at all times and in all situations. This can only lead to better health and human liberaation—for men.

PREDICTIONS AND SOLUTIONS

*There is a goal but no way; what we call
the way is only wavering.*

FRANZ KAFKA

*In America today men of affairs are not so
much dogmatic as they are mindless.*

C. WRIGHT MILLS

THE SOLUTION to the many problems of the corporate wife may be to
eliminate her. The concept of nonperson status—whether as executive
wife or as Johnny's mother—must be buried, for the sake of men as
well as women.

The demise of the corporate wife should bring no more grief than
the disappearance of the organization man, for whom Roger M. D'Aprix
has written the obituary: "The organization man is dead, a victim of
changing values and eye-opening events. I doubt that anyone will mourn
his passing."[1] D'Aprix envisages an extension of traditional limited goals
so that executives and corporations serve the needs of people and society as well as those of the firm. If the rumors of the organization man's
death are true and not a Mark Twainian exaggeration, one of the first
beneficiaries of the legacy must be wives. If there is no organization
man, there can be no corporate wife. For the latter, with the inequities
and penalties attendant on her role, was surely a creature of the aggressivity and *machismo* of the former.

Corporations that have taken the executive wife for granted either
as an unavoidable nuisance or as helpful "baggage" are warned that
such attitudes must be relegated to the museum of the outworn and
outmoded. This is the caveat of Professor James C. McDermott, of the
Fordham University Graduate School of Business Administration:
"More corporations had better start taking notice of the executive wife,

because increasingly she is the third party in most of the decisions made between her husband and his company. More companies will discover that one of the reasons they lose or cannot attract good managers is that they are not involving the wife in corporate decisions affecting her husband and subsequently herself."[2]

Unless employed and paid by the corporation, managers' spouses will increasingly refuse to be handled as appendages or commodities in the way they have been and regrettably too often are still today. The marriage partner, she or he, will have an independent ego and destiny and will act to fulfill them, with concomitant regard for the needs of the corporation. In the future wives or husbands of job candidates or employees will not be examined, inspected, screened, or tested either by hiring executives or by psychologists. And they will not be tyrannized by the spouses of upper corporate managers.

The future breed of spouse will be neither submissive nor obstructive. Individual human beings will maintain attitudes and behavior consonant with their own personal growth and fulfillment.

At a pace that few anticipated, corporate wives are gaining the assertiveness to demand an active voice in their destinies. Whether because their awareness has been raised by the Women's Liberation movement, or because they have been exposed to more of the world through travel and literature, they are today better prepared than even a decade ago to protest their manipulation. Their growing sense of independence has led them to question certain corporate practices, such as moves that are forced on them, compulsory entertaining, and the ubiquitous business trips of their husbands.[3] Both a cause and an effect of this independence is that a growing number of them now work—women who have been homebodies for years are now employed or are pursuing further schooling.

Even now the question of whether or not a woman should stay at home is beyond arguing. It is no longer an issue of whether men want it that way. Some 33 million women are presently in the workforce, with a fair number of them as the sole support of families. Women are fleeing the house en masse, largely in search of personhood, which in our society means having a piece of the public action. Women are in effect ringing the death knell to the societal requisite that they play solely the traditional role of wife and mother.

There will be other dramatic changes wrought of the new awareness that is just emerging in our lifetime. These changes will affect corporations and corporate functioning as they will all of society. For the prison of rigid role playing, masculine and feminine, will be replaced by a new, exciting concept of role sharing.

Mates will be full persons in their own right. No longer will the doctrine enunciated by Blackstone in the 1760s govern male-female relationships: "By marriage, the husband and wife are one person in law; that is, the very being or legal existence of the woman is suspended during the marriage, or at least is incorporated and consolidated."

Our society and our corporations in particular have been operating on that principle. The principle isn't working. As of this writing one-third of the marriages in America, apparently based on this misguided missive, now end in divorce, and the hidden casualties of the unions that survive are becoming increasingly known to psychiatrists, ministers, and marriage counselors. Human beings relegated to nonpersonhood just do not do well. Increasingly, people will not submit to their own undoing for the sake of others—whether spouses or corporations.

It is inconceivable that an educated, sensitive woman will do for her husband's company what, as the divorce rate indicates, she is unwilling to do for him. The quest for self-fulfillment and equality is the principal cause of marital breakup today. When wives accepted the submissive role that society assigned them, marriages were stable and lasted forever. Whatever the combination of factors motivating them, women are leaving their traditional role and are seeking personhood—full participation in all those civil and human rights that our civilization has cherished and that up to now have been the privilege of men, albeit a relatively few fortunate men. This is not a rush to unisex but rather a protest against the inferior status that for too long has been thrust on women.

Women have a separate historical past that enables them to make a distinct and salutary contribution to society. The difficulty has been that their desire to make this contribution has been stymied and thwarted by the denial of their basic rights and the failure to acknowledge their intelligence. The loss has been inestimable to society, which has been deprived of their wisdom; to men, who have had to adopt unnatural, distorting postures of "masculinity"; and to women themselves, who have suffered the diminution of spirit that comes with perpetual anonymity.

With the raised consciousness of this generation of women and with their new knowledge of their own capabilities, it would seem incredible that they could ever again accept the exclusion that has characterized their existence.

In the future, just as it is now unthinkable to employ a man without the promise of opportunity for growth and enhancement—or less than this, without some acknowledgment of personal worth—so it will not be expected that women or wives will dutifully accede to male or corporate decisions concerning them without similar rewards. Our be-

153

haviorists, despite all their repressive misconceptions, have made the valid point that a system of just rewards has the best chance of moving or guiding human behavior.

What were the rewards all these years for corporate wives? Vicarious ones at best and hardly compensatory for the undeserved penalties. This state of affairs could exist only with the denial of personhood for women. It was assumed that women didn't need personal rewards because they weren't considered people. This is a major reason housewives today are not compensated economically—neither salaried nor eligible for social security on their own.

In the not too distant future, corporate decision makers will be faced with the bittersweet necessity of taking the achievement motivation of both mates into account when recruiting or transferring employees. There will be some colleague marriages, with husband and wife having equal training and credentials as technical specialists or business executives. In some instances corporate America will be seeking out the wife as the executive, with the husband in the role of spouse. In all such cases the marriage partner will have to be placed as well, either in the same company or in a nearby concern.

To paraphrase President Kennedy: the company will ask not what the spouse can do for the company but what the company can do for the spouse. It will be the corporations that will be screened to see whether they can give opportunities for both people instead of the other way around. Regarding the corporate wife, in place of the docility and submissiveness that has been demanded of her, she may henceforth be judged on her achievement and productivity—if indeed she is to be judged at all.

For a glimpse of the possibilities of things to come, it is most instructive to look at some forecasts made by William J. Goode, professor of sociology at Columbia University.[4] He is optimistic about a woman's ability to perform at high managerial levels but is pessimistic about opportunities for advancement, because male managers will continue to place obstacles in her way, using the established clichéed rationalizations to cover their prejudice. Professor Goode sees no contradiction or dislocation in her being able to run a family and a corporation at the same time. He reasons that management is "inherently and organically a woman's job." Indeed she is trained in human relations. He predicts that women will produce better because of their learned ability to command and care for subordinates through persuasion and participation.

He foresees top-level female managers married to top-level male managers since people tend to choose spouses whose class and status are the same as their own. Female managers will continue to have children but will not be enslaved to their care. Our present system of child rearing, he comments, is an inordinate burden on women that is probably both unnecessary and counterproductive. He quotes sociologist Alice Rossi's observation that ours is the first civilization "to transform the socializing of children into a 24 hour job and it has been given to women."

Will children of working mothers suffer from lack of love or parental guidance? Professor Goode agrees with many other social scientists in feeling that especially in upper-middle-class homes, children will actually do better with somewhat more neglect than they now experience. And it will be advantageous to the whole family for the father to take a fair share of the burdens and joys of child rearing.

If women now unemployed enter the job market in significant numbers, will this not ultimately displace male workers, despite the comparison Sylvia Porter drew between married women jobholders and unemployed men in 1971? At some distant future date, it might, given no upswing in the economy and zero population growth. But social advances, as pointed out before, do not occur without adjustments of the status quo. The solution will ultimately come in the reduction of hours at work for all. Most of us will become in fact part-timers, getting our work done in less time than at present. Thus we will be talking about working fathers as we now do about working mothers. What we are to do with the freed time is another matter.

These are only a few aspects of the revolution—to use the frightening word of the last decade—that historical and contemporary forces are loosing in human society and specifically in the domain of women's participation in worldly activities. The nominating conventions of 1972, where women were in greater evidence than ever before in our political history, presaged things to come. The events of Miami Beach, projected into millions of homes, will have a prescriptive effect on the concepts of women's roles in areas of life far from politics. After watching their effectiveness and power at the conventions, no executive officer or personnel director will again be able to deny a woman an executive opportunity without twinges of guilt and self-consciousness.

But what of the practical problems of wives who do not wish to seek independent corporate recognition? What of the wives who must continue to pack and dutifully make the 10 or 12 moves that may ultimately mean the disintegration of their identity? Are we to write them off as ongoing casualties of an unjust struggle? Hopefully not. Ways can be found to lighten their burdens. Accommodations can be made to help preserve their identities.

For one, as indicated in previous chapters, there are families who would welcome relocation rather than abhor it. They might be transferred instead of those for whom moving entails hardship. It should be simple to discover who would like to move: all qualified employees could be informed of a job to be done in another area. Moving the family that welcomes the opportunity would then meet both company and personal needs. This would eliminate the present paradox complained of by numbers of young executives—the surest way to guarantee staying put is to make it known that you would like to relocate, and vice versa. In addition many more corporations might follow the lead of those described in Chapter 5 and actively consult rather than order their personnel whom they wish to transfer. Refusals should not be automatically taken as indications of uncooperativeness and subsequently penalized. Using human approaches such as these, corporations need not fear an image of softness but may indeed reap an unexpected dividend of increased morale and esprit de corps.

There are families in which the business trips of one spouse are not unwelcome to the other. Psychologist John Elliott says that in instances where there are two dominant or two submissive personalities, the traveling of one partner can contribute to the happiness and success of the marriage.[5] His conclusions can be confirmed, though he does not elaborate and his choice of descriptive terms may be questioned. (The woman whom he calls "dominant" may be merely autonomous—simply not looking to her husband's presence as the be-all and end-all of existence.) Given that the conventional marriage usually follows the male dominance–female submission model, a nondominant husband feels as much pressure to be assertive as does his wife to submerge her own leadership capacity. Separation is often a liberating experience to both. He can stop playing leader, and she is then free to express her own nature.

Granted that there are sharp limits to free choice in these matters, no one can deny that there is plenty of room short of anarchy for alternative ways of handling job assignments and business trips that would be entirely consistent with the movement toward humanizing corporate life. Sociologists Lionel Tiger and Robin Fox describe the pressing need of employees to see the leaders of vast, bureaucratic organizations as human beings rather than as faceless commanders of everyone's destiny.[6] Consultation on issues directly connected with the worker's life would go a long way toward this goal.

Corporate America has operated on the premise of increased efficiency, productivity, and growth. Perhaps this is how it had to be: the achievements have been spectacular in terms of accumulation of wealth, power, and an elevated standard of living (in the material sense) for

156

some. But hidden cost factors seem to have gone unrecognized. As we saw in Chapter 5, David Rockefeller has pointed to a "social audit" that will be made in the future—an assessment of the contributions and costs of business practices to human welfare.

We know that many men have grown rich and powerful. At the same time have we ever been conscious of how many wives and children were destroyed in the process, of the carnage of·burned-out spirits that success has left in its wake? These are hidden costs that we have been loath to face. Perhaps we are on the threshold of an era of humanization in corporate America when in Paul Goodman's idiom personnel will become people.

A primary target, if we are to see that era, must be the abatement of our frenzied mobility. And there are indications that the moving mania is being checked. A recent survey found that only 37 percent of executives expect to be moved every three years, down from two-thirds in 1970.[7]

Technological advances may make a complete reversal of this uprooting mania possible in the near future. New methods of communication such as cable television may obviate the necessity for on-the-spot contacts and surveillance. An example in contemporary politics of the use of presently available media is the debates of candidates separated by thousands of miles. Long-distance meetings and seminars are already being held over closed-circuit electronic networks. A professor or a diplomat can deliver a televised lecture to a group of listeners who can then speak to the lecturer by a long-distance telephone hookup. Human gatherings hopefully will never be completely replaced by such remote contacts but merely cut down to allow executives and their families to plant roots. Although it may be true that there is no substitute for being on site oneself, there is little doubt that the moving and traveling we now do is excessive. And if we can kick the habit of compulsive traveling our technology will enable us also to buy, sell, consult, supervise, and trouble-shoot—without leaving town.

To ameliorate the despair and loneliness of those who must play the waiting game, there are no universally adaptable solutions. Instead we must embrace a panoply of innovations to rehumanize the corporate wife.

One solution to the problem of loneliness, known to past generations and now revived by some members of the counterculture, is as unacceptable to general middle-class sensibilities as it is reasonable and workable. The solution is of all things living with other people who are also fighting loneliness. We knew and accepted this antidote in the era of the extended family, when parents, grandparents, and other relatives lived together and gave support and comfort to one another. Then the absence of a spouse was not a calamity. There was no need for police dogs and complex lock systems to achieve feelings of safety and well-being. This life style is gone now except in the roundly maligned experiments of the young, who give comfort to one another in communes and similar group-living accommodations. But many of us are too proud to learn anything from the young.

Yet regardless of the source or inspiration, adventurous people are in fact coming together, and middle-class people at that. Swallowing pride and snobbery they are carrying out their realization that human communication is more important than the preservation of a private turf. Cooperative living is catching on "among professionals, middle-aged workers, and otherwise 'straight' Americans."[8] In contrast to communes, which are usually located in rural areas, these cooperatives are found predominantly in urban areas. Several dozen are now in operation in and around Boston for example.

A principal reason for their growing popularity is the economic factor—a cooperative provides a standard of living that individuals otherwise could not afford. Furthermore it discourages robbery; someone is always there to deter intruders. Added advantages are that children and housewives are exposed to a wide variety of people and experiences, and there is never a dearth of babysitters. And of course the communal life combats simple loneliness. A 64-year-old widow is quoted as saying, "It seems that without a family of my own, I was considered practically useless." This would apply as well to many temporary corporate widows.

Although there have been numerous problems, as would be expected in any group of people with diverse backgrounds and without experience in cooperative living, this life style is becoming increasingly popular. People are beginning to fight back against isolation and social deprivation.

In this connection Alvin Toffler sees "situational grouping," a term coined by Dr. Herbert Gerjudy, as one of the key social arrangements of the future.[9] Such cooperative arrangements are recommended for people who have been subjected to uprooting and relocation and who are suffering from threats and anxieties that are similar because they are due to the stresses of similar social disruptions. Coming together would provide them with the opportunity to share both experiences and endeavors to cope. These situations would be temporary for most families, but others, needing group living on a long-range basis, would maintain the life style by preference.

Should an executive and spouse accept the idea of one remaining behind if the other finds a transfer irresistible or impossible to turn down, dual domiciles can be established. People of good will might indeed amicably arrange a marriage confederation so that inordinate sacrifices by either need not be made. Spouses who choose to live in different cities for a while or permanently because each has something important to do in a different place will not engender resentment in each other. And since human relationships are not at their most passionate either intellectually or physically when proximity is constant, dual residences may in fact be just what modern marriages need. A professional man told me that with respect to his wife, "Partings are not partings, and reunions are not reunions." A little less presence might cure such a situation. Navy wives, whose lives are made up of partings from their husbands, have discovered this compensatory side of the coin: "Lengthy separations are clearly no fun but the reunions which follow are like second honeymoons and help your marriage stay young through the years."[10]

Establishing dual residences to solve the problem of conflicting interests cannot be considered an optimal arrangement. For obvious reasons such an accommodation is made with great difficulty and sacrifice. And needless to say, it will be feasible for only an adventurous few. A handful of brave souls, calling themselves "jet set" academics, are attempting this double life. A report on them describes one wife: "On weekends, the long-haired 27-year-old professor lives with her husband in Cleveland. But on Monday she flies to New York, where she teaches English three days a week at Columbia University."[11] This is Bonnie Wheeler, who freely admits that she has a life of "controlled chaos" in which she spends her entire year's salary to pay for her commuting and her New York apartment. But "I take to that kind of chaos. I think I would be bored otherwise." Other couples live on separate campuses, though these instances are infrequent among those who have children. The report also notes that academic husbands are more likely "to reverse their traditional roles and tag along after their wives when the women are offered choice, high-paying jobs on campus."

The life style of separate locations offers a viable alternative for people of good will that may soon find its way into corporate America. Hopefully they will not be castigated or penalized for their innovative attempts to free themselves from our conventional imperative of togetherness—a togetherness that is more myth than reality, thanks to the traveling of the modern male executive. As many a corporate wife privately confides, the moves that are ostensibly made to keep the spouses together drive them farther apart. Wives and families are transplanted to form a new base of operation for husbands to be away from.

Why be married if you are going to be separated? Many women again reply that they have often asked that question of themselves.

Separating domiciles of course raises the problem of image. It doesn't look good; corporation eyebrows lift in concert when the wife doesn't move with her husband. At the very least marital disharmony is suspected. But most of all his executive capabilities come under question; how will he be able to command others when he apparently has so little authority over his own wife? This is the corporate *machismo* that places a premium on tyranny and penalizes humanness. Indeed to be a real man, a real executive, a person should not have to *command* anyone. We may evolve to a state where true manhood will be measured by the ability to yield to the reasonable needs of others and where yielding will not be thought of as weakness, effeminacy, or irresponsibility.

When the full history of the institution of marriage is written, it may emerge that much of the time and energy devoted to it was misspent and actually detrimental to mental growth and happiness. Much of what we now consider love and devotion may in another age be viewed as demanding of servility and an animal dependence. Just as we in the 1970s are embarrassed on seeing the rerun movies of the 1930s and 1940s on television because of their simpleminded sentimentalities, our present clinging notions about marriage may similarly be embarrassing to our grandchildren.

Serious thought is being given to ways to modify the traditional marriage contract. In an article titled "A Radical Guide to Wedlock," Norman Sheresky and Marya Mannes undertake to spell out what a modern agreement might be.[12] They would turn sentimental vows into a legal document, finding that at present Americans marry with less knowledge of what they are doing "than when buying a car." Yet the attitude of the state is that marriages "are not to be lightly discarded, even if they have been lightly contracted."

The authors draw up a hypothetical premarital contract containing nine articles to be agreed to by both parties. Article I is a declaration of marital intention—that both people are entering into matrimony freely and without coercion. Article II, called "Historical Representation," contains disclosures by both about their past history, including health records, obligations, earning capacity, sexual ability and proclivities, education, and nature of ties and hangups with relatives and others. Article III, dealing with "Future Expectations," is particularly relevant to the thrust of this book: the prospective wife and husband agree that the place where they are to reside shall be determined by proximity to *his* place of business, regardless of where she may be employed and "regardless of whose earnings are greater." Here clearly is a departure

160

from Women's Liberation attitudes, the man being given priority and advantage. This provision is consistent with traditional attitudes, hardly a radical notion as the title of the essay claims.

Another unradical and indeed sexist proposal pertains to sexual fidelity. Both parties state that they oppose adultery. He indicates that on learning that she had committed adultery, he will immediately divorce her. She on the other hand hedges. She will judge the circumstances of the occurrence. If it is a "meaningless" episode, she would rather not even know about it. Here again is the traditional double standard. The male is under no condition to be cuckolded. Yet he is given permission to play around a bit if he is discreet.

Although one can validly argue about the content of these guidelines, the idea of an explicit and even legalized agreement must be deemed a giant step forward. Candor is undoubtedly helpful, but given conditioning and the inordinate pressures of love and longing, people may willingly agree to stipulations that will lead to frustration and disillusionment. Therefore more than candor and confession are necessary to insure a modicum of justice and fair play in the conjugal contract.

In their best-selling book, *Open Marriage,* Nena and George O'Neill offer a blueprint of a truly new life style for couples. They contrast the traditional marital arrangement and expectations (closed marriage) with what might be (open marriage). In the traditional contract they observed the following:

Clause 1: Possession or ownership of the mate. (Both the husband and the wife are in bondage to the other: "You belong to me." Belonging to someone is very different from the feeling that you belong *with* someone.)

Clause 2: Denial of self. (One sacrifices one's own self and individual identity to the contract.)

Clause 3: Maintenance of the couple-front. (Like Siamese twins we must always appear as a couple. The marriage in itself becomes your identity card, as though you wouldn't exist without it.)

Clause 4: Rigid role behavior. (Tasks, behavior and attitudes strictly separated along predetermined lines, according to outdated concepts of "male" and "female.")

Clause 5: Absolute fidelity. (Physically and even psychologically binding through coercion rather than choice.)

Clause 6: Total exclusivity. (Enforced togetherness will preserve the union.)

These are the expectations and results implicit in the present-day contract; at the time of marriage, their consequences are rarely anticipated. The ideas are homilies of a past day. Their perpetuation in modern life

161

has contributed to the feelings of boredom, loneliness, and despair that seem to overwhelm so many married people.

As a replacement for these clauses, the O'Neills offer the open marriage contract: "Undependent living, personal growth, individual freedom, flexible rules, mutual trust, expansion through openness." The realistic expectations of open marriage are

- that you will share but not everything;
- that each partner will change—and that change can occur through conflict as well as through a gradual evolvement;
- that each will accept responsibility for oneself and grant it to one's mate;
- that you cannot expect your mate to fulfill all your needs or to do for you what you should be doing for yourself;
- that each partner will be different in needs, capacities, values, and expectations because he or she is a different *person,* not just because one is a husband and the other a wife;
- that the mutual goal is the relationship, not status, or the house by the sea, or children;
- that children are not needed as proof of love for each other;
- that one should *choose* to have children, undertaking the role of parent knowingly and willingly as one of the greatest responsibilities in life;
- that liking and loving will grow because of the mutual respect that an open relationship engenders.[13]

Underlying the suggestions for the new life style is the concept of egalitarianism in human relationships. But to some readers the *open* marriage contract may seem excessive, shocking—too great a departure from what we have known. To others it may seem ineffective; they would argue that until women are socially and economically liberated and are no longer dependent on husbands for food and status and shelter, talk about open marriage contracts is premature. There is truth in this. However strong the good intentions of the parties involved, it is difficult indeed for two people who are grossly unequal in the outer world to form an egalitarian union in their inner world. It is for this reason that Norman Sheresky and Marya Mannes' "radical" marriage contract is actually almost amusingly sexist.

Despite this criticism, their proposals, like the O'Neills', perceptively highlight the crucial need to reshape the marital relationship. In the final analysis this is a question of substance rather than form. As long as women, children, and men are attempting to live joyfully together, it matters less whether the setting is a monogamous union, a commune, or any other arrangement, than whether each treats the other as a person—not a pawn. Martin Buber enunciated this principle in his I-thou model. He decried the I-it relationship that is so characteristic of a competitive society and urged people to relate to each other as humans, not as objects. Paul Tillich expressed the same vision in preaching love with justice.

The Greeks felt that love could exist only between men—love between equals. Perhaps our generation can contribute to the world ethic by submitting a model of love between men and women—love between equals.

As summary, this author turns to the perceptive statement of Jessie Bernard in her book, *The Future of Marriage:* "Men and women will continue to disappoint as well as delight one another, regardless of the form of their commitments to one another, or the living style they adopt, or even of the nature of the relationship between them. And we will have to continue to make provision for all the inevitable—but, hopefully, decreasing—failures of these marriages to meet the rising demands made on them which we can unequivocally expect."

REFERENCES

PROLOGUE

1. *The Dairy of Anaïs Nin,* Vol. 3, 1939–1944 (New York: Harcourt Brace Jovanovich, 1969), p. 215.
2. Charles Reich, *The Greening of America* (New York: Random House, 1970), p. 80.

CHAPTER 1

The opening quotation is from *The Diary of Anais Nin* (Vol. 3), p. 87

1. Myrna M. Weissman and Eugene S. Paykel, "Moving and Depression in Women," *Transactions/Society,* July–August 1972.
2. Lois Wyse, *Mrs. Success* (New York: World, 1970), pp. 136–146.
3. Charles Reich, op. cit., p. 295.
4. Quoted by George Vecsey in *The New York Times,* June 15, 1972.
5. This and the following letter were printed in *The Wall Street Journal,* February 28, 1972.

CHAPTER 2

The opening quotation is from *The Imperial Animal* (New York: Delta, 1972), p. 135.

1. Vance Packard, *A Nation of Strangers* (New York: McKay, 1972), p. 5.
2. William H. Whyte, Jr., "The Wife Problem," in Robert F. Winch and Lois Wolf Goodman, eds., *Selected Studies in Marriage and the Family* (New York: Holt, Rinehart and Winston, 1968), p. 187. © *Life* magazine. Reprinted by permission.
3. *The New York Times,* June 15, 1972.
4. Richard Reeves, "Nixon, Inc.—Corporation-Style Politics," *New York Magazine,* September 4, 1972.
5. Quoted in Whyte, op. cit., p. 182.
6. Nancy Shea, *The Air Force Wife* (New York: Harper & Brothers, 1951), p. 6.
7. *Life,* April 28, 1972.
8. "The Women of the Men Who Serve," *Paul Harvey News,* February 15, 1972.
9. *The New York Times,* June 28, 1972.

REFERENCES

CHAPTER 3
From the poem "Prelude" in *Western Star* (New York: Farrar & Rinehart, 1943).

1. Vance Packard, *A Nation of Strangers* (New York: McKay, 1972), pp. 187–188.

CHAPTER 4
Christopher Morley's statement can be found in his book *John Mistletoe* (Garden City, N.Y.: Doubleday Doran, 1931). The quotation from Thomas Szasz is from his book *The Second Sin* (Garden City, N.Y.: Doubleday & Co., 1973).

1. Quoted in William H. Whyte, Jr., "The Corporation and the Wife," *Fortune,* November 1951.
2. "What Moving Means to the Family" (Boston: Children's Hospital Medical Center, ND), p. 5.
3. Urie Bronfenbrenner, "Raising Your Children," *Today's Health,* June 1972.
4. "What Moving Means to the Family," p. 12.
5. Quoted in *Medical Tribune,* November 10, 1971.
6. T. S. Eliot, *The Cocktail Party,* act 2, in *The Complete Poems and Plays* (New York: Harcourt, Brace, 1952), p. 364.
7. Josephine W. Johnson, "My Civil Disobedience," *The New York Times,* May 10, 1969.

CHAPTER 5
The quotation is from "The Corporation and Society in the 1970s," *Reflections,* Vol. VII, 1972, p. 51.

1. Alan N. Schoonmaker, *Anxiety and the Executive* (AMA, 1969), p. 71.
2. *The New York Times,* May 1, 1972.
3. *The Wall Street Journal,* September 13, 1972.
4. *The Wall Street Journal,* May 30, 1972.
5. *The Wall Street Journal,* February 28, 1972.
6. Schoonmaker, op. cit., p. 65.
7. William N. Christensen and Lawrence E. Hinkle, Jr., "Differences in Illness and Prognostic Signs in Two Groups of Young Men," *Journal of the American Medical Association,* vol. 177, pp. 247–253, 1961.
8. *The New York Times,* June 9, 1972.
9. *The New York Times,* September 24, 1972.
10. *The Wall Street Journal,* October 10, 1972.
11. William H. Whyte, Jr., "The Corporation and the Wife," *Fortune,* November 1951.

12. Alice Lake, "I Hate My Husband's Success," *McCalls,* July 1958.
13. Quoted in C. G. Rogers, "Executive Wives Gaining New Status," *McCalls,* August 1971.
14. Ester Wier, *What Every Air Force Wife Should Know* (Harrisburg, Pa.: Stackpole, 1966).
15. W. R. Roberts, "Executives, Wives, and Trouble," *Dun's Review,* January 1965.
16. Ninka Hart Burger, *The Executive's Wife* (New York: Macmillan, 1968), p. 135.
17. William H. Whyte, Jr., "The Wife Problem," in Robert F. Winch and Lois Wolf Goodman, eds., *Selected Studies in Marriage and the Family* (New York: Holt, Rinehart and Winston, 1968), p. 177. © *Life* magazine. Reprinted by permission.

CHAPTER 6
The opening quotation was found in a *New York Times* feature story, June 4, 1972.

1. William H. Whyte, Jr., "The Wives of Management," *Fortune,* October 1951.
2. William H. Whyte, Jr., "The Corporation and the Wife," *Fortune,* November 1951.
3. William H. Whyte, Jr., "The Wife Problem," in Robert F. Winch and Louis Wolf Goodman, eds., *Selected Studies in Marriage and the Family* (New York: Holt, Rinehart and Winston, 1968), p. 178. © *Life* magazine.
4. Robert Townsend, *Up the Organization* (New York: Knopf, 1970), p. 62.
5. *The New York Times,* April 29, 1973.
6. Sigmund Freud, *Civilization and Its Discontents* (New York: Norton, 1962), p. 27.
7. Alice Lake, "I Hate My Husband's Success," *McCalls,* July 1958.
8. Lois Wyse, *Mrs. Success* (New York: World, 1970), pp. 59–67.
9. *The New York Times,* June 4, 1972. © 1972 by The New York Times Company. Reprinted by permission.
10. Whyte, "The Wife Problem," op. cit., p. 177.

CHAPTER 7

1. Erich Kahler, *The Tower and the Abyss* (New York: Braziller, 1957), p. 41.
2. *The Village Voice,* April 12, 1973.
3. The following case history is reproduced, with permission, in slightly adapted form from Robert Seidenberg, "Fidelity and Jealousy: Socio-Cultural Considerations," *The Psychoanalytic Review,* Winter 1967.
4. Connie B. Howes, "Job Travel Isn't Glamorous for Him—or Her," *Today's Health,* September 1970.

5. The following case history is reproduced in slightly adapted form from Robert Seidenberg, "Interpersonal Determinants of Reality-Testing Capacity," *Archives of General Psychiatry,* vol. 3, 1960, p. 368.
6. Philip E. Slater, *The Pursuit of Loneliness* (Boston: Beacon, 1970), pp. 68, 9 and 74.
7. *The New York Times,* August 3, 1972.
8. Alice Rossi, "Family Development in a Changing World," *American Journal of Psychiatry,* vol. 128, 1972, p. 1057.
9. Reported in *The Los Angeles Times,* August 21, 1972.
10. *The New York Times,* April 29, 1973.
11. *Life,* March 17, 1972.
12. Thomas Szasz, *The Second Sin* (Garden City, N.Y.: Doubleday, 1973), p. 52.

CHAPTER 8
Alan Dugan's couplet is from "Speech for Aeneas," *Saturday Review,* January 30, 1965.

1. *The New York Times,* April 16, 1972.
2. J. Anthony Lukas, "The Alternative Life-Style of Playboys and Play-mates, *The New York Times Magazine,* June 11, 1972.
3. Rollo May, *Love and Will* (New York: Norton, 1969), p. 58.
4. Lukas, op. cit.
5. *The New York Times,* April 30, 1972.
6. Lois Wyse, *Mrs. Success* (New York: World, 1970), p. 98.
7. Ibid., p. 91.
8. The following case history is reproduced, with permission, in slightly adapted form from Robert Seidenberg, "Older Women and Younger Men," *Sexual Behavior,* April 1972.
9. John Barnett, "The High Cost of Success," *Science Digest,* October 1967.
10. William H. Whyte, Jr., "The Wives of Management," *Fortune,* October 1951; "The Corporation and the Wife," *Fortune,* November 1951.
11. Karen DeCrow, *The Young Woman's Guide to Liberation* (Indianapolis: Bobbs-Merrill, 1971), p. 142.
12. Robert Townsend, *Up the Organization* (New York: Knopf, 1970), p. 116.
13. *The New York Times,* August 27, 1972.

CHAPTER 9
Up the Organization

1. *Herald-American Post-Standard* (Syracuse, N.Y.), July 23, 1972.
2. *Herald-Journal* (Syracuse, N.Y.), May 22, 1972.

3. *The Wall Street Journal,* September 21, 1972.
4. *The Wall Street Journal,* October 2, 1972.
5. *The New York Times,* August 6, 1972.
6. *Herald-Journal* (Syracuse, N.Y.), September 29, 1972.
7. *The New York Times,* July 16, 1972.
8. *The New York Times,* November 5, 1972.
9. Vivian Gornick, "Why Radcliffe Women Are Afraid of Success," *The New York Times Magazine,* January 14, 1973.
10. The following case history is reproduced in slightly adapted form from Robert Seidenberg, *Marriage in Life and Literature* (New York: Philosophical Library, 1970), Chap. VI.
11. Jack Olsen, *The Girls in the Office* (New York: Simon & Schuster, 1972).
12. *The New York Times,* July 16, 1972.
13. *The Wall Street Journal,* September 8, 1972.
14. *The New York Times,* September 9, 1972.
15. Quoted in *The Wall Street Journal,* March 20, 1972.

CHAPTER 10

The quotation of Franz Kafka is from *The Great Wall of China* (New York: Schocken Books, 1936), p. 283; that of C. Wright Mills is from *The Power Elite* (New York: Oxford Press, 1956), p. 356.

1. Roger M. D'Aprix, *Struggle for Identity: The Silent Revolution Against Corporate Conformity* (New York: Dow Jones–Irwin, 1972), p. 106.
2. Quoted in George J. Berkwitt, "Corporate Wives: The Third Party," *Dun's Review,* August 1972.
3. Ibid.
4. *The New York Times,* December 26, 1971.
5. Quoted in Connie B. Howes, "Job Travel Isn't Glamorous for Him—or Her," *Today's Health,* September 1970.
6. *The Imperial Animal* (New York: Delta Publishing Co., 1972), pp. 118–148.
7. *The Wall Street Journal,* October 10, 1972.
8. *The Wall Street Journal,* July 7, 1972.
9. Alvin Toffler, *Future Shock* (New York: Random House, 1970), p. 385.
10. Anne Briscoe Pye and Nancy Shea, *The Navy Wife* (New York: Harper & Row, 1965), p. 6.
11. *The New York Times,* November 13, 1972.
12. *Saturday Review,* July 29, 1972.
13. Nena O'Neill and George O'Neill, *Open Marriage* (New York: Evans, 1972), pp. 67–88. Copyright © 1972 by Nena and George O'Neill. Reprinted by permission of the publisher, N. Evans and Company, Inc.

169

SELECTED READINGS

The titles listed below are recommended in addition
to those listed among the references.

Abbott, Sidney, and Barbara Love. *Sappho Was a Right-On Woman*. New York: Stein & Day, 1972.

Bernard, Jessie. *The Future of Marriage*. New York: World, 1972.

Chesler, Phyllis. *Women and Madness*. Garden City, N.Y.: Doubleday & Co., 1972.

Goode, W. J. *World Revolution and Family Patterns*. New York: Free Press, 1963.

Gornick, Vivian, and Barbara Moran, eds. *Woman in Sexist Society: Studies in Power and Powerlessness*. New York: Basic Books, 1971.

Janeway, Elizabeth. *Man's World, Woman's Place*. New York: Morrow, 1971.

Josselyn, Irene M. *Adolescence*. New York: Harper & Row, 1971.

Kanowitz, Leo. *Women and the Law,* Albuquerque: University of New Mexico Press, 1969.

Keniston, Kenneth. *The Uncommitted, Alienated Youth in American Society*. New York: Delta, 1965.

Mill, John Stuart. *On the Subjection of Women*. Greenwich, Conn.: Fawcett, 1971.

Millett, Kate. *Sexual Politics*. Garden City, N.Y.: Doubleday & Co., 1970.

O'Neill, William L. *Everyone Was Brave*. Chicago: Quadrangle Books, 1969.

Pierson, George W. *The Moving American*. New York: Knopf, 1972.

Rockefeller, John D., III. *The Second American Revolution*. New York: Harper & Row, 1973.

Sampson, R. V. *The Psychology of Power*. New York: Pantheon, 1966.

Seaman, Barbara. *Free and Female*. New York: Coward, McCann and Geoghegan, 1972.

Szasz, Thomas. *The Manufacture of Madness*. New York: Harper & Row, 1970.

INDEX